Military House Hacking

How to Earn Passive Income

and Create Generational Wealth

Second Edition

Markian Sich - Michael Foster - Eric Upchurch

Adam La Barr - Timothy Kelly - Mitch Durfee

Paperback ISBN: 979-8-9851790-0-2
Hardcover ISBN: 978-0-692-19778-3
eBook ISBN: 979-8-9851790-1-9

Dedication

We would like to dedicate this book to the courageous men and women of the United States Armed Forces—past, present, and future. Because of their sacrifices we can embrace liberty, the ability to pursue happiness, and the right to earn financial freedom.

"I serve with the memory and pride of those who have gone before me, for they loved to fight, fought to win, and would rather die than quit." - NSDQ

Table of Contents

Foreword

When Markian and his team asked me to write the foreword for a book that was being written for the purpose of becoming a valuable financial resource for members of the US Military, I jumped at the opportunity. I am honored and humbled to speak to the value and importance of this book for members of our esteemed military.

I am traveling in Italy and France as I write this, remembering what our military did to help these countries in World War II and the ultimate sacrifices many of our soldiers gave to keep our world safe from tyrants.

The courageous and valued members of our military are trained to be warriors, but they, like most people in our great country, are not trained to be financially successful. This simple yet very valuable book bridges that gap.

I have owned over two thousand homes and apartments buildings so far in my real estate investing career. I'm the host of the number-one multifamily real estate podcast in the world, "Lifetime Cash Flow through Multifamily Properties," which at the time of this writing has been downloaded over four million times. I am also the author of the book, *How to Create Lifetime Cash Flow through Real Estate Investing*. I say this only to lend credibility to my next statement:

If you are presently in the military, or have been in the past, and you know you want and deserve more financial freedom for yourself and your family, then you must read this book and connect with the Active Duty Passive Income team and community.

You must learn how to utilize the incredible lending opportunities our government has provided to our military. The VA Loan Program was established to help our military members become homeowners but can also be used to help you create financial freedom for yourself and your family. And that is only one of the many tools explained within these pages.

Study this book, connect with this team, push through any financial fear that you must, and take massive action with what you learn here.

You deserve it.

With deep, sincere gratitude,

Rod Khleif

Introduction

Military Real Estate Investing™ is a process where those who have served our country in the Armed Forces past or present, apply their unique, hard-earned military benefits to real estate investing strategies that can accelerate their financial success.

More specifically, Military House Hacking™ is an investment method by which an active duty service member or veteran can become a homeowner, a real estate investor, and a landlord all in one small accessible deal. By implementing strategic investment principles with a primary residence, it is possible to reduce or eliminate living expenses altogether.

This Book is Not for Everyone

Let us get one thing straight: I loved serving in the US Marine Corps, the United States of America, and everything that this country has provided for my family. My government paycheck was more than enough to cover my living expenses, and we even got to take some great vacations on our own dime. However, since I discovered real estate investing a few years ago, I've been on an unstoppable, steady track to break the military's financial mindset; to influence our brothers- and sisters-in-arms; to teach them what my team and I have learned and applied, and how they, too, can reach financial freedom through real estate investing.

This book serves as an important introduction to that mission. Because many people are focused on traditional investment strategies, this book will not be suited for everyone. In fact, this book may not be accepted by some military members and veterans. They may avoid it. They may even reject it.

Why? The structured nature of the military is not conducive to the development of an entrepreneurial mindset. And that is OK! Our military has one key focus: to protect and defend our nation at all costs. If service members start getting too distracted by earning money elsewhere—following side-hustle strategies or passions that fall *outside* of their military responsibilities—a part of their daily work ethic and concentration on the mission could fall to the wayside. That concept is a threat to both a traditional military way of life and common investing and retirement strategies that are being taught.

The question I asked myself many years ago was: Is there a way that military service and entrepreneurship can complement each other? This thought morphed into: Is there a way I can actively set myself up for a more comfortable and stress-free transition into the civilian world while still on active duty? This book explores these questions and provides some appealing solutions.

Before you are done reading this book, you will be convinced that it *is* possible to become a military entrepreneur by investing in real estate. If done correctly, it could enhance your effectiveness within your military occupation, make you incredibly wealthy, allow you to retire earlier, and open a door to a behind-the-scenes view of our country's financial "engine room."

Military House Hacking is not going to give you all the answers. It will serve as a catalyst to get you started, but its purpose is to introduce thought-provoking concepts so you can *choose* to take the next step.

When you are ready to take action, be sure to connect with us at www.activedutypassiveincome.com. We have curated dozens of resources, trainings, free content, helpful relationships, financial services, and accountability groups to ensure you can take decisive action when you have committed to creating the life you deserve.

- Markian Sich

The Test:
Is This Book Right for You?

Throughout our military careers we are taught to be winners in battle and in training. We are expected to be squared away at home and in all facets of our lives.

So, why aren't we taught winning financial strategies as well?

Our military structure demands uniformity to instill discipline and to guarantee measurable results in training and in war. However, like a powerful tornado, military uniformity is a relentless force that can sweep financial wisdom away and plop it down in the same time slot as a run-of-the-mill, four-day-weekend, holiday safety brief. Military financial education has become more of a checklist procedure within a PowerPoint presentation. Learning how to manage money is often considered to be one of the stereotypical external difficulties — a distraction — in our lives that the military forces into a box; uniform and simplified so as not to distract from the mission.

You can just sense the non-entrepreneurial mindset as soon as you check into your first unit:

"You aren't experienced enough to manage your finances and you don't have the time to learn how to invest wisely!"

"Just put your money away in the TSP and do your job!"

"Don't you dare buy an expensive car outside of base!"

"Don't get a credit card, you will never get out of debt!"

Sound familiar? Good or bad, it is the same old mindset and content. Instead, what we are taught is an abbreviated, over-simplified version of some financial guru training on TV or radio.

Our military structure suffers from an age-old epidemic of financial illiteracy. The current, feeble attempt at a financial education strategy is inadvertently insulting our intelligence by boring us with ineffective financial death by PowerPoint sessions. The military mistakenly grooms our service members to worry more about saving money than becoming wealthy. I'll reiterate and emphasize an important point: this is OK! It's not the government's job to teach us how to become wealthy. Active Duty Passive Income (ADPI) is here to change that landscape forever.

So here is the test to know if this book is for you. Answer the following questions below:

- Have you ever found yourself brainstorming for a way you could earn another stream of income?
- Have you ever felt like the only financial wisdom you have received is always focused

on saving more, reducing expenses, all for the hope you will be able to retire when you are sixty-five?

- Have you ever, *even for a second*, thought about how nice it must be for your landlord when they collect their rent checks from you?
- Have you ever felt a little awkward or restrained when someone insinuates that wanting to be wealthy is a bad thing?

If you find yourself answering Yes to any of these questions, then reading this book will feel like scratching an insatiable itch. It will quench your thirst for learning how to expand your financial horizons while on active duty, separated, or retired.

This book will *not* provide an answer to all your questions, but that is the point. It is meant to create a spark within that will get your gears turning and will make you question patronizing, antiquated financial advice.

Now, let's break through. It is time to focus directly on a *new* mindset and strategy that can pull you out of the rat race and into a life where you can create generational wealth for your family. Let's calculate your Military Financial Freedom Number™.

Exercise: Military Financial Freedom Number

Do you know your Military Financial Freedom Number? This is an exciting way to really understand how to set your financial goal for retirement, instead of just hoping to save some arbitrary amount over $1,000,000 in your IRA or Thrift Savings Plan (TSP). It will help you calculate how many rental properties (or some other cash-flowing asset) you will need to own to generate enough monthly passive income to retire comfortably. Ideally, the goal is for your passive income to meet or *exceed* your total monthly expenses. When this is accomplished, you are truly financially free. When you reach this number, you can stop working completely and your financial needs will still be met each month.

This exercise will provide a clearly defined picture of what your exact financial goals in retirement could be. But first, let's ensure what is meant by the word *retirement*. When real estate investors say retirement, we do not typically mean sitting around on a rocking chair on your porch. You will find that the real estate investing crowd sees the word as a pleasant and rewarding outcome derived from achieving one's financial freedom number. Hence, we use the term *financial freedom* almost synonymously with retirement or to mean *I'm able to do whatever I want now.*

If you decide to step into the world of real estate investing and become a part of the ADPI community, knowing your financial freedom number is crucial. So, let's get yours calculated, written down, and placed in a visible location. This is not only your goal; this exercise is the first step toward reaching your dreams.

Part 1: Calculating Your Military Financial Freedom Number

Step 1: Calculate your last three months of expenses across all your credit cards and bank accounts. You can leave out any major or unusual expenses, such as a new car or a 90" TV you bought after deployment. Your expenses should include housing (rent or mortgage), car payments, retirement deposits, internet, phone, utilities, restaurants, groceries, entertainment, etc. This should include all expenses that are recurring and necessary.

Step 2: Divide your total number by three to get the average of the three months.

Step 3: Your Military Financial Freedom Number equals that three-month average, multiplied by 1.5, and rounded *up* to the nearest thousand.

EXAMPLE:

Three months, total expenses = $13,666.68
Three-month average = ($13,666.68)/3 = $4,555.56
$4,555.56 x 1.5 = **$6,833.34**
Then, round the result up to the nearest thousand.

Military Financial Freedom Number = $7,000

The $7,000 in this example represents how much money would be needed every month to achieve financial freedom, financial independence, or retirement. You multiply the number by 1.5 (or increase it by 50 percent) simply because it's a good idea to be extra conservative so you have enough to buy that occasional TV, go on vacation with your family, or feel comfortable knowing you can pay all your bills if a financial anomaly occurs.

Part 2: Calculate How Many Assets You Will Need

Now it's time to calculate how many rental properties you will need to achieve that goal. Later in this book, we will explain some strategies to get you there, so keep reading!

Expenses will vary asset to asset, but on average your monthly net income should be positive. The positive income that remains after *all* expenses have been paid is what real estate investors call *cash flow*.

Your goal is to purchase enough rental properties (assets), so the combined total of your properties' cash flow reaches or surpasses your monthly Military Financial Freedom Number.

Let's stick to our figure of $7,000 from our previous calculation to keep the numbers easy.

One strategy discussed later in this book, is to buy a house, duplex, triplex, or fourplex at each duty station as you move around the country. Prior to buying one of these owner-occupied primary residences at each duty station, you must first scrutinize its income potential. You must consider that each "home" you purchase has potential to be a future investment property. You will run an easy-to-learn financial analysis to ensure it can produce a net-positive income if/when it does become a rental.

Action Item: To reach an educated, prior military, investment-savvy agent or lender anywhere in the US, reach out to our team at www.activedutypassiveincome.com/connect.

In the example below, we will say that our minimum desired cash flow is $250 per month, per property. This is achievable in most markets and even in most economic cycles if you know how to analyze a deal and you are willing to be patient and sometimes apply some creativity.

In locations where the market simply will not produce a high enough positive cash flow from a primary residence-turned-rental, you can shift your focus to purchasing properties in other markets. This is common and many investors choose to start with out-of-state (OOS) property investing. These assets may be in the form of turnkey rental properties, which isn't hacking necessarily, but can be a great asset to add to your portfolio. This strategy works best if you have enough money for the down payment, or if you can partner with friends and family to get the deal done. You may never live in some of these homes, or even see them in person, but real estate investors are okay with this. We view our rental properties like mini businesses, so it's important to be agile.

Now, let's do the math.

There is only one step in this calculation: Military Financial Freedom Number divided by average monthly cash flow.

Our example: $7,000/$250 = 28 rental properties

If your Military Financial Freedom Number and the subsequent number of properties seems like an unattainable number to you, keep reading. By the end of this book, you will see that purchasing rental properties can become a part of how you reach your goal. It is a path to financial freedom that has been followed by many service members before you. Moreover, there are many ways to accelerate the number of properties you own. You could scale up, diversify asset classes, or simply use the cash flow to pay off the mortgage on fewer properties, increasing monthly cash flow drastically.

If you want to see a more thorough explanation of how you can achieve this before you retire from the military, go to: (https://www.youtube.com/watch?v=MvNdU ZkfcuM).

Do your own calculations below right now. It should not take you more than five minutes. As soon as you calculate your number below, go to our Facebook Group (www.militaryrealestateinvesting.com), which is home to tens of thousands of active duty, veterans, and their families, and post your result! We will be watching for it!

1. Three months total expenses = $ _____

2. Total expenses/3 = $ _____

3. Three-month average x 1.5 = $ _____

4. Lastly, round that number up to the nearest thousand.

Military Financial Freedom Number = $ _____

Before we dive into strategies, however, let's discuss some financial fundamentals that will supplement your success. We want you to have all the resources we wish we had when we got started in the military. It's our duty to ensure you are armed to do this the right way. To help you succeed, we must establish a financial education baseline.

Good Debt and Assets

Let's get ready to decode the differences between assets and liabilities and good versus bad debt. It's important to provide a basic understanding of these two concepts to ensure the rest of the content is as effective as possible. It will also serve as the basis for creating the right mindset needed to become a successful real estate investor.

A simple definition for assets and liabilities are: An **asset** is something that *increases* your net worth (puts money in your pocket each month). A **liability** is something that *decreases* your net worth (takes money out of your pocket each month).

For example, a car is almost always a liability. Unless you purchased a muscle car in the 1960s and kept it in a garage for the past 50+ years, it is not likely making you any money. In fact, the value of a car is likely depreciating, *and* you are paying for it every month – not good. It does have a purpose of course; to get you from point A to point B, but it is most likely not in the asset column unless you made a net profit at resale. Even then, it would still be labeled as more of a potential asset as you use it. The only other way that you could consider your vehicle an asset is if you choose to walk or bike to work and rent your car to someone else (or buy a fleet of vehicles to rent out). Many people have started doing this with companies like Turo, which is like AirBnb for vehicles.

On the other hand, a great example of an asset would be a solid cash-flowing rental property. A property that has tenants paying off your debt and generates a positive net cash flow every month, is an asset. It puts money *in* your pocket, after all expenses, each month. It could be argued that with real estate investing, a property is not an asset unless it cash flows (produces more money each month than its operational expenses).

Example: If a mortgage is $2,000 a month and you are only receiving $1,500 in rent every month from the tenant(s), that property is stifling your lifestyle instead of enhancing it. It's more of a liability at that point than an asset. It might have potential to produce a net profit at resale in five to ten years, but it's not producing cash flow each month. In this scenario, you are paying to own the property each month, which defeats the purpose of buying an asset for cash flow.

Most real estate agents and lenders who work with service members are not properly educated on how to buy primary residences from a military perspective. They are not often trained to look at a property as if it will likely become a rental at some point in the future. Because of this, many military members (most of the ADPI team included) end up with negative cash flow when they PCS or move.

A point-of-view that could present a lasting problem is if an owner treats a rental property that does not have a monthly positive cash flow as an asset, simply because of the net gain in equity each month. It may be technically true, and that debt-reduction is one important pillar of investing principles, but it is a slippery slope for a real estate investor to think this way.

Cash flow should always be viewed as a paycheck. You are trying to create passive income and establish financial security and freedom for your family. Do not be tempted to ruin the best part of real estate investing by putting your hard-earned money into a property that decreases your cash flow or relies on appreciation. Cash flow is our primary investment goal. We *never* invest solely for potential appreciation. If that happens, it's just icing on the cake, but it's not the strategy to rely on.

Another problem that we see happen often is people start to fear debt so much that they try to pay a property off as quickly as possible. This is *not* always the best solution.

There is a crucial difference between good and bad credit, and here's why:

- **Good debt** is debt that enables you to purchase an asset.
- **Bad debt** is debt on a liability.

In other words, good debt makes you more money than it costs you every month — a net positive cash flow. Bad debt is simply taking money away from you.

You should get excited about good debt and shy away from bad debt. Sometimes, however, our lifestyle requires us to accept bad debt, like that new (or used) car purchase we mentioned above. This is where many people fall into another peculiar mindset trap and act emotionally.

If you have bad debt that is a very low interest rate, it may not be the best strategy to pay it off early! Why? In short – opportunity cost. Because you could make the extra money that does not go toward paying off the debt, work for you by turning it into an asset. It may not make sense to throw that extra money into paying off something that is already a liability if you can instead use it to buy an asset — we will discuss this more in depth in the bonus chapter, Blueprint to Financial Success.

For example, if you buy a car for $20,000 at a 4 percent interest rate, it will cost you roughly $361 a month to pay it off over a five-year period. That comes out to about $1,660 total in interest paid. What if instead of paying cash for that $20,000 car (because you have an emotional aversion to purchasing depreciating liabilities now), you invested $20,000 into an asset that earned you 8 percent interest annually?

You would instead *profit* by $1,660 after just the first year of investing that same $20,000! Moreover, you have the remaining four years to pocket that extra income and determine your next investing opportunity. Or if having that new car ever becomes a necessity, you have now increased your net worth and your ability to afford it.

Now that you understand the basics on assets, liabilities, and good and bad debt, let's talk about some strategies, starting with military house hacking.

Military House Hacking: Goodbye Living Expenses!

As we defined earlier, the intent behind house hacking is to reduce or eliminate living expenses altogether. If you are flexible, creative, and are knowledgeable on how to correctly analyze the property, you might even make a net profit each month. By incorporating your unique military benefits and following some basic methods outlined in this book, you can become remarkably successful at military house hacking, while serving our nation.

What's also exciting is that it is not required to be on active duty to house hack. Later, you will learn about some common civilian practices (for those of us who have separated from service), as well as out-of-the-box strategies our team has implemented as veterans. Military house hacking provides a lifetime of opportunity at your fingertips once you understand these principles.

As alluded to previously, we will not discuss in detail how to save a dollar here and there by eliminating life's simple and sometimes necessary pleasures. The purpose of this book is not to explain frugality or all the things you should not be doing. Instead, it is more impactful to discuss ways to improve your day-to-day lifestyle by eliminating or reducing one of your biggest monthly expenses than explain how to invest your newly liberated money into assets that will increase your income.

Before we get into specific strategies of military house hacking, let us identify that biggest expense each month: the cost of housing. Since our focus is going to be on reaching your financial freedom number as rapidly as possible, we hope you have already started shifting your mindset from saving money, to investing it. If you can reduce or eliminate your largest expense, you can invest that money, instead, into income-producing assets.

Rental properties, for instance, are an asset class that can cash flow very well and have multiple ancillary benefits (taxes, appreciation, loan reduction/increase in personal net worth, leverage, hedge against inflation, to name the most prominent). If you compound the cash flow and other perks from owning multiple properties over time, things start to get exciting.

Unless you live below your means, or someone is letting you live with them for free, it's a good bet that your housing cost is higher than any of your other revolving, monthly expenses. Think about that for a second. Many people learn to simply accept these expenses as inevitable.

You and your spouse may enjoy going out to dinner frequently. But that cost is still no comparison to your housing expenses, which far exceed your restaurant and other leisure expenses combined. This is an important point to make because many people have a strange rationale when trying to save money. Some people may try crazy things like switching to a Ramen-only lunch diet. They do this just to save $50 every week. You can't blame them too much; learning to be frugal — an extreme saver — is being taught rampantly in the United States.

A saver mindset:

- Save money on small everyday pleasures and put that extra cash into a retirement fund
- Constantly worry about how much your debt is costing you over time
- Painfully cut out more of life's pleasures every time new expenses arise in your life (like the cost of raising children or saving for their college tuition)
- Compare prices on everything

If you were brought up to have a saver mindset as most Americans were, you may have found yourself thinking about how big of an impact that $50 would make over time. Let's flip the table and execute a truly impactful strategy of investing instead of trying to painfully reduce our everyday pleasures by strategically applying an investor mindset.

An investor mindset:

- Cut out your biggest expenses and invest that difference into assets that produce cash flow

- Take that newly produced cash flow and incrementally invest it into more cash-producing assets
- Save money for the sole purpose of *investing*
- Love good debt that costs little and is used to purchase high-yielding assets

Challenge yourself to do three things to shift from a saver mindset to an investor mindset:

- Create/discover more streams of income or cash to invest (side hustle, real estate, tax returns, work bonuses, inheritance, etc.)
- Eliminate or reduce your biggest expenses (housing expenses) and invest that money in assets that create more income
- Focus on educating yourself on this topic. Abe Lincoln once said, "Give me six hours to chop down a tree and I will spend the first four sharpening the axe." Sharpen your mind in the same way!

If nothing else, eliminating your housing expense first will render immediate and impactful results in your lifestyle. More importantly, it will allow you to invest that money and *exponentially* increase your income.

Once you have made the decision to shift your mindset, you can then begin taking action by implementing strategies that allow you to pursue your financial freedom number.

There are at least a dozen ways to house hack, but this book is committed to explaining tried and true methods of house hacking specifically for military members, veterans, and their families. Only two-tenths of 1 percent of the world's population are eligible to take advantage of some of these methods. The strategies here, if pursued aggressively, could accelerate your timeframe in reaching your Military Financial Freedom Number and goals.

This is what you need to get started for a traditional approach to military house hacking while still serving:

- Knowledge (we have you covered here)
- Two to four years' time, or one to two duty rotations in the military
- Veterans Affairs (VA) Loan eligibility, or some startup capital for a Federal Housing Administration (FHA) loan (more on these later)
- A well-defined strategy
- To never lose sight of the goals you created

Next, you will need to understand how to evaluate a potential investment property. Let us cover the fundamental two-step process that almost all real estate investors use as a baseline analysis when looking for an investment property.

The 1% Rule

This rule requires the monthly rent for the subject property to be no less than 1 percent of the purchase price. It serves as a great back-of-the-napkin method to analyze a potential deal, so you can decide quickly whether to pursue it further.

The 1% Rule takes two elements of a property into consideration: the purchase price and the potential rent. To see if a house is a worthy rental property, simply divide the potential rent by the purchase price.

Note: it is a great idea to talk to property managers in the area to gauge your level of accuracy on potential rent values. There are also resources like Rentometer.com that can give an estimate of what to expect.

Example:

- Potential monthly rent: $1,000
- Purchase Price: $110,000
- 1,000/110,000 = **0.9 percent**

As you see in this example, this property would *not* meet the 1% Rule (the result was only 0.9 percent); the monthly rent is less than 1 percent of the purchase price. It *could* still be a great rental, but we would need to take the analysis a step further to really see the property's full potential. You might want to ask for more information from the broker/agent, request a tour of the property, get inspections done, receive repair bids from contractors, look at job diversity and market population growth, look at local schools, and more.

In continuing the evaluation, you would run a more detailed analysis for your expenses. These expenses can be summarized by an easy-to-remember acronym.

PITI-PMMV - This is the acronym often used to describe the total out-of-pocket monthly expenses for an investment property. Ideally, the rent you collect monthly from the tenant(s) will be greater than the total PITI-PMMV value.

Monthly PITI-PMMV expenses are:

- Principal - debt to the bank
- Interest - cost to borrow from the bank
- Tax - property tax, often between 1 to 2 percent of the value
- Insurance - property liability insurance
- Property Management - a fee to a third-party company, typically between 7 to 10 percent of the rental monthly income for leasing, rent collection, managing repairs and upkeep, evictions, and more
- Maintenance (repairs) - typically 5 to 10 percent
- Vacancy - typically 5 to 10 percent (this includes average tenant turnover times between leases)

When you find a property that meets the 1% Rule (or is as close as you feel comfortable, based on your deeper analysis), you would then subtract the PITI-PMMV total from the rental income to reveal your monthly cash flow value. If the result is a net positive number, you likely have found a property that is a great investment.

So far, you have learned what is considered an asset, how to shift your mindset to that of an investor, and how to evaluate a potential good investment. Next, you will learn how to take advantage of some of the most commonly applied, but rarely taught, investing strategies and tools that military members — past and present — can use.

Like any good education, the best place to start is by building a foundational base layer. Understanding the VA Loan can be one of the most essential elements to both getting started and scaling up.

The VA Home Loan

Active Duty Passive Income recognizes and reinforces that the Veterans Affairs Home Loan (VA Loan) can be one of the best resources for service members, past and present, and their families to get started with real estate *investing*, so we wanted to take extra care and attention when writing this chapter.

The intent behind the content you are about to read is to arm you with knowledge that will further your journey toward financial freedom and make a lasting impact in your family legacy. You will learn the basics about the VA Loan that will dovetail nicely with investing strategies and methods that the ADPI community has successfully employed repeatedly and with intention, which are explained in this book.

Note: The VA Loan was not created specifically to be used as an investment tool and is, and always has been, an owner-occupied loan product. All regulatory guidelines from the VA and individual lenders must be closely followed when using this product. To connect with an approved lender, please contact the ADPI team.

One of the most useful benefits a service member can receive is lifetime access to the VA Loan to purchase a primary residence. This is a federally backed loan product that boasts competitive interest rates, with no down payment requirement, yet demands no private mortgage insurance (PMI). Using the VA Loan can also allow service members to start leveraging equity (maybe even cash flow) in a home or primary residence, which can then help build generational wealth for their family.

Why is this so exciting? Leverage is one of the most powerful wealth-building tools in America; buying a home with the VA Loan, smartly and with intention, can maximize leverage, eliminate common barriers to entry, and help keep some hard-earned cash in the pockets of our service members.

Additionally, if the principles taught by ADPI are applied properly and within the guidelines of the VA and lender, the purchase of a single-family home, duplex, triplex, or fourplex with a VA Loan could also become an excellent cash flowing investment.

Buying a home with the VA Loan can be one of the most important decisions in a service member's life. If not done properly, with care, and diligence, a home purchase could become more of a liability than a future asset—and we see it all the time, which is one reason ADPI has assembled this and many other resources.

Finding the *right* home to purchase as we PCS around the United States (or after service, as a veteran) can come with challenges if not analyzed correctly, but it could also simply not be a wise investment. With the right education and support, the ADPI team, based on personal application, believes that there is almost always a deal to be found if the right strategy is applied. And the VA Loan can help.

What Exactly is a VA Loan?

First off, the VA is not a lender; it does not provide loans to service members. A VA Loan is a loan that is *backed* by the United States Government, specifically the Department of Veterans Affairs, which comes with its own set of guidelines. In other words, it's a loan that, once initiated, approved, and processed, is federally backed.

But what does that mean and why is that important?

If a homeowner defaults on that loan, the VA is guaranteeing to pay the bank up to 25 percent of the original loan amount lost in the transaction. That is a major benefit to a lender. Because of this, lenders should be *more* willing to give you a new home loan if they know that there is a (VA) guarantee.

There are some qualifications that you must meet on several different fronts, which will determine your eligibility for a loan, as discussed below. Once you have proven eligible, connected with a lender, and obtained a pre-approval, you can meet with a real estate agent and begin the buying process. You can connect with an agent and lender on our resource page at the end of this book.

Note: it is not required to be preapproved before working with an agent, but it's highly recommended.

The vetted, investor-savvy agents and lenders that work with the ADPI community can guide you through the process and can help you find a property that fits your investment strategy, budget, and personal goals.

The reality is, going through the process of purchasing a new home can be very stressful. Even though you have a federally backed loan product, it does not mean the seller of the home you want to purchase will care (more on that later); they might still simply be looking for the highest price offer. So, throughout the homebuying process, stay the course, manage emotional expectations, focus on the long-term result, be prepared for some stress, and make sure your first step is finding a fantastic lender and agent team to get you to the finish line.

The Benefits of the VA Loan

After we clarify all the benefits of the VA Loan, you will realize what a shame it is that less than 13 percent of service members who are eligible for the VA Loan take advantage of this incredible tool.

The Primary Benefits of a VA Loan Are:

- **No Down Payment** - One of the most fascinating things about the VA Loan is the no down payment option. When you use a conventional loan to buy a home, they will require a down payment between 3 and 20 percent of the purchase price. Depending on the size of your home, this could be more money than you have on hand. With the VA Loan, you *can* put money down (i.e., to manage the monthly payment amount or reduce the funding fee), but it's not required.

- **No Mortgage Insurance** - Another great benefit of the VA Loan is that you aren't required to pay private mortgage insurance (PMI). If you pay less than 20 percent of the purchase price as a down payment with other loan types, you must also pay mortgage insurance. This extra payment — which uses insurance to "hedge" the risk from the lender to the borrower on higher risk loans — can add significantly to your final monthly payment amount. PMI will protect the lender if you are unable to make the payments on your home. Since the VA Loan does not require PMI, you can save substantially.
- **No Prepayment Penalty** - Often, veterans use the VA Loan to get started with their first primary residence. Whether PCSing, changing job locations as a veteran, upsizing or downsizing properties, or using military house hacking strategies, there won't be a penalty for paying back the VA Loan early.
- **Different Loan Types** - The VA offers fixed or adjustable rates and can be used for several different types of home loans, as discussed below.
- **Easy to Qualify** - The barrier to get a VA Loan is one of the lowest in the industry. The VA guarantees the loans up to a certain threshold, meaning that if you default on the loan, the

bank will still get part of their money back. This makes lenders more likely to offer loans to eligible vets even with lower credit scores than conventional lending would allow and even borrow more.

- **Choose your lender wisely** - Different lenders and brokers will offer different rates for VA Loans. Be sure to connect with a vetted, knowledgeable, and experienced military-focused lender.

Now you understand why the VA Loan product is great, but how do you know if you are eligible for a VA Loan?

VA Loan Eligibility

Determining VA Loan eligibility is the first step when beginning the process. The Department of Veterans Affairs has established a set of criteria, both **service-related** and **financial**, which determine whether the veteran or service member is eligible to buy a home using the VA Loan. The lender, separately, has criteria that must be met.

Here are some essential documents that you might be required to present to a lender when you begin the process:

- **DD Form 214** - A "DD214" is a document given to a veteran when they end their active-duty service. It shows where they served and what kind of discharge they received when they left the military. This discharge information is imperative as those with a

"Dishonorable" discharge status are ineligible. [If you are still active, in lieu of the DD 214, you will need to apply for a Certificate of Eligibility (COE) from www.ebenefits.va.gov or you can apply by mail VA form 26-1880.]

- **VA Form 26-1880** - Form 26-1880 is a request document for a Certificate of Eligibility (COE). Obtaining a COE is another step that will be necessary in the loan pre-approval process. This is simply a letter from the VA that lets the lender know that you meet all the VA requirements to receive access to using the loan product. A good lender will help the veteran or service member get their COE.
- **VA Form 28-8937** - Form 28-8937 may be needed for those who have service-disconnected disabilities that could require adaptive modifications to be completed on the home. For example, if your new home needs to have an access ramp installed, this would incorporate that cost into the loan amount to be financed with the purchase of the home.

VA and Lender Requirements

As mentioned above, the VA has service-related and financial guidelines of their own that must be met. Their standards will determine your connection (or your spouse's connection in some circumstances) to the military service along with how long you served. Once again, your discharge information is going to be necessary. Your discharge status could mean the difference between receiving eligibility or not.

VA's Guidelines for Service-Length Criteria:

- Served ninety consecutive days during wartime (just reduced in 2021 for guard to thirty days)
- Served 181 of active service during peacetime
- Obtained a minimum of six retirement points while reservist or guard member
- Spouse of a veteran who died in the line of service

Once you have met one of the above requirements and have all your financial documentation in hand, this is when you would apply for your Certificate of Eligibility (28-1880) described above. This certificate can be obtained through the VA, or if you choose a VA-approved lender, they can take care of the COE for you. Using a qualified lender can make the process much more comfortable.

You can also find all the documents you might need through ebenefits.va.gov or VA.gov; you will just need your login information to access them. Another method is to send all your applications and paperwork through the mail, but this takes much longer. If using the mail, you will need to have all documents sent with signature approval and be sure to make copies in case they get lost or damaged.

It should be no surprise that the banks will also have some standards that must be met once you have hopped over all the VA's hurdles.

Bank/Lender Standards That Must be Met:

- **Minimum Credit Score** - The lender will determine a credit score that you must meet before moving on. This is a tricky step for some homebuyers and could often mean months or years of credit repair work before they are able to purchase their next home. Typically, a minimum 620 FICO is expected (but some lenders can go down to 500 if certain conditions are met). If you need help repairing, maintaining, or building your credit, please feel free to use our credit resources at www.activedutypassiveincome.com/resources.

- **Steady Income** - Having a job at a single employer for at least the last two years is advised before getting into the buying process, but not mandatory in all cases. Steady income shows the lender that you can make enough income to afford the payment on the home loan.

- **Debt-To-Income Ratio (DTI)** - Your debt-to-income ratio is calculated by taking all your monthly bills divided by your monthly income (before taxes). This ratio is reported as a percentage. For example, if your monthly bills are $1000 and your monthly income before taxes is $4000, your DTI would look like this:

$1000/\$4000 = 0.25$ or 25 percent. Your ability to fit the mortgage payment into the rest of the bills is important. Typically, for a VA Loan, a lender will look for a 69 percent DTI or better. Anything below 43 percent is optimal. There are some exceptions, and a good lender will walk you through this process.

Once these standards have been met, you should be able to begin searching for your new home. You should also note that there will still be various fees involved in the loan closing process. If you can negotiate that the seller covers the closing costs, it will save you a lot of money.

Advantage of a VA Loan Offer

"My agent said sellers probably won't accept my offer because it's a VA Loan and I'm not putting any money down."

Sound familiar?

Below is an education piece regarding VA buyers you can use that may help you (and/or your real estate agent) explain to a seller and their agent or broker, as to why your VA Loan offer can be a *better* option for them to consider. It may or may not sway the seller's decision, but this, coupled with information provided below, could certainly help.

Here is an example letter:

"My client, Mrs. XXXX, has submitted an offer on your property. I'm sending you this letter to kindly ask that you take careful consideration when it comes to reviewing their offer.

Not only are they excellent, well qualified, and preapproved borrowers, they are also a United States Service Member [or veteran], willing to lay down their life for our great country. For this sacrifice, they have earned access to an excellent home loan.

Contrary to what you may have been told in the past, the VA Home Loan is one of the **easiest and most secure loans** to close in our industry. As an approved VA Lender, [insert lender name] is able to ensure that these loans close quickly and smoothly.

Some important facts about VA buyers and the VA Home Loan process:

average **FICO**	clear to **CLOSE**	appraisal **VALUE**	oath to **SERVE**
712 SCORE	**21** DAYS AVG	**2** MORE OPTIONS	**0%** DOWN EARNED

- The average veteran home buyer has a credit score of 712.

- At [insert lender name], VA purchases receive a "Clear-to-Close" on average in 21 days or less.
- VA appraisals have more flexibility than Conventional and Federal Housing Administration (FHA) loan appraisals, with two additional opportunities to come to value, allowing all parties to work together to override an appraiser's opinion of value.
- A veteran's time served protecting our freedoms is their "skin in the game". Their ability to purchase a home with a federally backed, no down payment loan is a benefit earned, not a potential risk to financing.

Sincerely,

[Name of REALTOR]"

Not only could you consider using some of these points to make an impact on a party involved in the transaction who thinks otherwise, but we believe every real estate agent in the United States should understand and implement this stance.

Types of VA Loans

Before you shop for a loan, it is important to consider what type of VA Loan product you might need. VA Loan types include: purchase, cash-out refinance, Interest Rate Reduction Refinance Loan (IRRRL), rehab, construction or Native American Direct Loan Program (NADL).

Deciding which is right for you is simple.

Typically, if you are looking to purchase a single-family home under or within your county loan limit, you will need a standard purchase VA Loan. If the property exceeds your county limit, it would be called a Jumbo VA Loan. Your lender will take care of this part, but it's good to know there is a difference.

Effective January 1, 2020, The Blue Water Navy Vietnam Veterans Act of 2019 made some important changes that could drastically improve a VA buyer's purchasing power.

Within the Act, Public Law 116-23 established that veterans and active-duty service members who have their full entitlement eligibility (i.e., they have no outstanding VA Loans) are no longer limited to, or capped by, county loan limits. For example, if a veteran is eligible, can afford, and qualify for a $2 million property, they can now receive 100 percent financing with no PMI.

Standard, conforming limits apply to those who are already using some or all of their VA Loan entitlement.

If you want to build new construction, you might need a VA construction loan, however not all lenders will provide these. It's common for veterans to get short- or long-term financing from the builder or recommended local financial institution, then to refinance into a VA Loan. If you are a Native American veteran or married to one, you may also qualify for the NADL to build, buy, or improve a home on Federal Trust Land.

If you want to buy a residential multifamily (two-four unit), you would use the same standard or Jumbo VA Loan, but you will need to consider potential financing limitations with your lender as specified by the VA. In some instances, a four-unit property with an included commercial space can be financed.

The VA Lenders Handbook (VA Pamphlet 26-7) also mentions a VA rehab loan that is for alterations and repairs. This loan is separate from the original VA Loan and can be simultaneously added at closing when the primary residence is purchased.

Refinancing a VA Loan

Refinancing with a VA Loan can be simple and effective. Not only does the VA allow you to purchase a home with their loan program, but they can also let you refinance a home and potentially even send some cash straight to your wallet. They have a couple options when it comes to refinancing, and each will either lower the interest rate or give you a cash option to make repairs or upgrades to the home.

The Two Types of VA Refinance Loan Are:

- **VA Streamline** - The Interest Rate Reduction Refinance Loan (IRRRL), often called the Streamline Refinance is just a refinancing product that allows the buyer to lower interest rates and take advantage of potential earnings, if available. One of the best things about the Streamline is that it is a loan that requires no out-of-pocket expenses, and no re-appraisal of the residence. There are some stipulations, however, which are discussed below in the interview with a lender.

- **Cash-Out Refinance** - A cash-out loan is for those homeowners who have built up equity and may be looking to make some repairs or additions to their home, want to pay off other debts, or just take cash out in case a good investment opportunity arises. This sounds like a home equity loan, but the difference is that the VA replaces your original loan, whereas a home equity loan is an additional loan atop your mortgage.

Whichever loan product you choose, these are some easy options that won't end up costing you a lot of money in the long run. One of the smartest things to do with a VA refinance is to create more buying power for future purchases. The refinance is a great way to build up equity and add value to your existing home at the same time.

Finding your eligibility level for a VA refinance is similar to what you went through to get the original VA Loan. You will have to provide your DD-214, with honorable discharge, and your financial records to show that you can afford the new rate. There could be some additional hoops,

50

so keep the documents ready for any eventuality that might come up.

Choosing a VA Lender: Where and How to Get a VA Home Loan

Performing a Google search for VA home loans returns almost 40 million results. That could be a bit cumbersome to sort through if you are starting from scratch. When looking for a lender there are a few things to know and understand about mortgage lending first, starting with the different types of lenders out there.

There are traditional banks, mortgage lenders, and mortgage brokers.

Traditional banks are where you hold your checking and savings account, and many will also finance a home. They tend to be convenient, but often you are just a number — one of thousands of files.

Mortgage lenders, like our preferred in-house ADPI lender, are neither too big nor too small. Personalized service with a great team to make sure lending is competitive with quality follow through.

Mortgage brokers are independent agents who are often working alone or with a small support team to negotiate with wholesale mortgage lenders all over the country. They can give you great one-on-one service, but without a larger team to help, you could run a small risk of your file being mishandled.

How experienced is the broker?

Working with someone who knows the process of buying a home with the VA Loan very well should be one of your first considerations. It can also be helpful if your loan officer understands the VA Loan not only from the lending side, but from first-hand experience. Finding a veteran loan officer can add an additional layer of knowledge — your loan officer will understand the realities of PCSing as well the technicalities of the lending process. Find someone who has built a reputation for knowing every inch of the home-buying process, but also buying with the VA Loan.

How fast is their process?

Turnaround time is vital in the buying process. Being able to have a signed contract and close with twenty-one to thirty days should be typical. If your lender has a slower time, they might be working with a larger firm that has more moving pieces to initiate the process. Be sure to ask this question so you know what to expect. The closing process could still take longer, but the lending piece should conform closely to this standard.

What is their interest rate?

As discussed earlier, the VA has different rates depending on individual lenders. This improves your chances of getting a better deal and saving thousands of dollars down the road. Checking a lender's interest rate is one of the most significant parts of the searching process. Ask what fees and overrides they charge to see if there is anything you can compare to other lenders.

Who are the processor and underwriter?

If you use a traditional bank, your loan officer might be calling you for business and taking your initial application, but from there it gets handed off to a more behind-the-scenes loan processor. Make sure when searching for a lender, you know who will be handling your paperwork throughout the process. On the other hand, mortgage lenders have a dedicated team, meaning your loan officer, processor, and underwriter are a cohesive team who work together throughout the process, all having hands on your file throughout the lending period.

Do they know their Section A?

It's critical that a lender knows how the Section A portion of the home loan works. Section A shows fees that could be due, from the buyer, at closing to pay for loan processing and other paperwork that could not be covered in the home loan. Nothing is worse than delaying a closing due to a lack of funds, so make sure to ask your loan officer and processor to explain in detail.

How easy is it to communicate with the lender?

Wouldn't it be nice if you could reach out at any time to your lender and speak with them? You can! Search for a lender who is at your disposal if any problems with financing or the home occur. Nothing is more frustrating than waiting on someone who is never around or difficult to contact.

Now that you know what to ask the lender, it is time to sit down and slog through a long table of results to see which company will work best with you. If you want a quick transaction, it would be best to work with a smaller to midsize company as they have fewer hands to pass through while processing the loan.

You can also reach out to us to expedite this process.

The Complete VA Loan Process

1. Get your "financial house" in order. Here's the blueprint to get you started.

2. Ensure your credit is where it needs to be to get the best rates.

3. Gather financial documents needed to close.

4. Choose an experienced VA-approved lender.

5. Complete lending application.

6. Get your Certificate of Eligibility (lender can help).

7. Get preapproved/prequalified with your lender.

8. Find an investor-friendly, educated, military, veteran, or military spouse real estate agent.

9. Start house hunting. Select your home or Military House Hack property. Write the offer.

10. Sign the purchase agreement.

11. Lender processes the loan application and locks your interest rate.

12. VA appraisal ordered by the lender.

13. Closing!

Interview with a Loan Officer

We interviewed Spencer Thomas, one of our in-house loan officers with almost twenty years' experience, to get his rapid-fire responses on some commonly asked questions about the VA Loan. Here is the transcription:

First things first: Why is the VA Loan so impactful to vets and Active Duty?

Response: Foot in the door, on average homeowners have 44x more net worth than renters, guaranteed by the US government, no down payment required, no mortgage insurance required like FHA, or conventional financing above 80 percent LTV.

Who is eligible for the VA Loan?

Response: Credit score as low as 500, time in service, or discharged for a service-connected disability. During war, that's ninety consecutive active-duty days served, (in) peacetime is 181 active-duty days served, active duty is ninety consecutive days, reservist or guard there are several factors, like six creditable years, but there is also a new Veterans Health Care and Benefits Improvement Act that includes eligibility after a thirty-day stint.

How do you get a Certificate of Eligibility?

Response: Log into eBenefits.va.gov and follow the instructions or, even easier, the ADPI lending team can help pull it for you.

Is it really 0 percent down?

Response: Yes, it can be. One hundred percent Loan to Value (LTV), but you might still have closing costs and a funding fee. The seller might be willing to pay for closing costs and the funding fee can be wrapped into the loan. And if you have a 10 percent or higher disability rating, the funding fee is waived.

Note: below is the latest VA Funding Fee chart for reference.

	If your down payment is...	Your VA funding fee will be...
First use	Less than 5%	2.3%
	5% or more	1.65%
	10% or more	1.4%
After first use	Less than 5%	3.6%
	5% or more	1.65%
	10% or more	1.4%

Source: va.gov

Can you do a Cash Out Refinance of a VA Loan?

Response: Yes. It can go up to 100 percent of the appraised value, but most lenders have better pricing at 90 percent Loan-To-Value or less. They also must occupy home as primary residence.

What is an interest rate reduction refinance loan (VA IRRRL)?

Response: The interest rate reduction refinancing loan is commonly called an IRRRL. It is just what it sounds like: a loan product to reduce the interest rate of a VA Loan. The IRRRL has a three-year recoupment rule that determines total monthly savings from new payment to old payment, divided into the actual costs incurred (VA funding fee, lender and title fees, but escrow creation doesn't count). It also has a half percent interest rate decrease requirement and must be at least 210 days from the date of the first payment or six months, whichever is longer.

How many VA Loans can a single service member or veteran have?

Response: There's no limit unless entitlement is maxed out. Starting in 2020 the cap went away but if a borrower has an existing VA Loan, then the easiest way to determine how much eligibility is left is to subtract the original loan amount from the conforming loan limit based on the county you are buying in. For example, the county conforming loan limit is $548,250 for a single-family home in most counties, and you obtained your previous loan for $300k, so then you have 248,250 left of a VA Loan amount to buy another home.

How many times can a single service member reuse their VA entitlement?

Response: If the homes are sold, there isn't a limit. There is a one-time restoration of entitlement. If a veteran refinances an existing home into a conventional or other non-VA Loan they can apply for a one-time restoration of entitlement. The thing to remember is that this is a *one-time* restoration so make sure to use it the best way possible. For example, if you have a VA mortgage on a home for $500k and you are PCSing to Virginia and want to buy a fourplex for $2 million on a VA Loan, you would first need to refinance that previous home into a conventional loan, pay it off, or sell it, to free up your entitlement. A poor example would be if someone refinanced a VA Loan for a $100k into a conventional loan and only wanted to buy the next home for $250k. In the last example the veteran had enough entitlement to carry both loans at the same time and wasted their one restoration.

What are eligible property types for the VA Loan?

Response: Single family, condos, townhome, manufactured, modular, and multifamily — up to four units normally, but can also buy a property with a commercial space attached to it as long as the commercial unit doesn't exceed 25 percent of the overall square footage.

What's the maximum number of units?

Response: Four, plus one commercial space if only using one VA entitlement. If two vets are applying together there are ways to exceed this if the lender doesn't have an overlay, but it is rare to find a lender that will accept this type of financing.

What is the VA Construction Loan?

Response: There are two main types of VA Construction loans: One is a One Time Close (OTC) VA Loan, meaning you get one loan at a fixed rate prior to the builder starting and your payments usually start once you can occupy the home. Another type is the more traditional construction loan that you get to finance just the costs to build the home, have usually purchased the land separately, and then once the home is completed you refinance all the debt into one VA home loan. Not many lenders offer VA Construction Loans. There are some caveats, such as it must be completed in nine months, or the land acquisition cost cannot exceed a certain amount, etc. In today's market of high material costs and lack of workers, it is likely in your best interest to find a home already completed to purchase. Once the market cools down a bit, a VA Construction Loan may be a better option.

What is the VA Renovation Loan?

Response: VA Renovation loans are not easy to come by these days and the lenders that offer them usually put many constraints on them, so much so that it is usually better to get a different type of financing. The constraints can be as simple as a maximum loan amount of $100K additional in renovation work or more complicated like you cannot do anything that affects the foundation or studs of the home. Other financing options that may be worth looking into are the FHA 203K Loan, which allows you to pretty much do anything to the property, including tearing down the home to the studs, or maybe a home equity line of credit [HELOC] if you have sufficient equity in the home and can pay it off sooner. Typically, according to the VA handbook, VA Renovation Loans are only meant for cosmetic type work and can't be used on more than two-unit buildings. This is a separate loan from the VA Loan, where the lender will let you borrow up to the new value of the home's ARV (After Repair Value) or the total of the costs to complete the work, whichever is lower.

Is there a limit to your VA Loan?

Response: Technically, no, unless you currently have an outstanding VA Loan. Most lenders, however, will cap you at $1.5 - 2 million, but we have seen VA Loans as high as $3 million. There is a per-county conforming loan limit that the VA will authorize funding or entitlement up to, then it's up to the lender to ensure the borrower still qualifies. If you currently have a VA Loan, it is important to determine how much entitlement you have left to use. The way to determine remaining entitlement is by taking the original loan amount on the current VA Loan(s) and subtract it from the conforming county loan limit in the county you want to purchase a home. As of today, most counties in the United States have a conforming county loan limit of $548,250, so if your original VA Loan was for $250K (doesn't matter what you owe on it now, only what the original amount was) then you subtract that from the $548,250, which equals $298,250 remaining of a loan amount you can borrow up to with no down payment required on the next home.

You can exceed the remaining entitlement amount if you are willing to put 25 cents per dollar that you exceed the entitlement. Using the previous example: If you wanted to buy a home for $300k, you would have to subtract the remaining loan amount of $298,250 from $300k, which equals $1,750, and put down 25 percent of that amount, which would be $437.50.

How much credit can you get at closing from the sellers?

Response: Four percent allowance for recurring and non-recurring closing costs that cannot go toward principal balance but can help pay down funding fee.

How do dual military spouses use their entitlements?

Response: If both entitlements are unused, only pick one spouse's entitlement to use. It is a good option to leave the other's free for future purchases without a cap, or you can use both as long as they have enough entitlement left.

What about unmarried co-borrowers? Split entitlements possible?

Response: If the lender allows it with permission of the VA, it is acceptable. And a non-veteran, non-spouse coborrower may be allowable if the lender allows it, and VA approves it. They would be required to put 12.5 percent down of the purchase price.

What's the maximum Debt to Income Ratio Requirement for a VA Loan?

Response: Most lenders will go up to 69 percent DTI on the back end.

What are the occupancy rules?

Response: The eligible borrower must intend to occupy within sixty days of closing, has to be a primary residence, it cannot be a second or vacation home, and cannot be an investment property. But if orders come in after closing and you have to PCS, for instance, it's ok. This can also be delayed if orders are delayed. If you find out that you cannot occupy the home within sixty days prior to closing, you must inform your lender and delay or cancel your closing.

Can I put my VA Loan home into an LLC?

Response: No, the VA Loan cannot be in an LLC. Sometimes you can retitle the property into an LLC, but you are technically not supposed to, and this could cause the lender to call the note due in full.

Can a VA Loan be used on an investment property?

Response: Not if the veteran will not live in at least one of the units. Remember, this is an owner-occupied loan product. If you have a property that you previously occupied and then turned it into a rental property, some lenders will allow you to still do a VA IRRRL even though it's not a primary residence anymore.

Can future income of a multifamily home count as income for the veteran?

Response: Yes, if the veteran has at least a year of landlord experience or a property manager that can be proven by tax returns or verification of employment of a property manager. And you can only count the units that will not be occupied by the veteran. The VA has made exceptions in the past by allowing a veteran without landlord experience to count future income if they are willing to sign at least a year contract with a property management company.

Can rental income be counted as income for veterans who want to obtain a new VA Loan?

Response: Yes, if rental income can be proven through tax returns and lease agreements for at least two years for each property. If the properties were newly acquired and written permission is given from the VA, the income from the properties may be counted if the veteran signs an annual contract with a property management company and has a current tenant under contract on the property.

Now that we have given you a look into what the product is, let us show you how to apply it!

Military House Hacking Strategies

Single-family VA Loan Hacking

The single-family hack, using the VA Loan, is perfect for those with little to no cash savings. It allows you to buy a decent home where you are stationed with a 0 percent down payment. You can even roll the VA Loan funding fee and closing costs into the loan.

A couple of notes to reiterate on the VA Loan; the VA Loan is an owner-occupied loan product. That is, the buyer must intend to live in the property they are purchasing. The original intention of the VA Loan is not to accumulate a rental property portfolio; however, as long as a service member or veteran follows VA guidelines and lender requirements, it can be an amazing tool!

While this might be great for younger, single, military members to get started, this method is not always perfect for married couples and/or families. The key element to this hack is renting out extra bedrooms to friends, family, or comrades. It could be perfect for a group of younger military members who receive Basic Allowance for Housing (BAH) or who would have rented a house or apartment together otherwise.

This strategy is a lifestyle decision, so consider your specific situation prior to jumping into it.

Many would benefit from using this strategy on active duty. For example: Markian and some flight school classmates became renters because they thought it would be easier. However, some students took a different approach. They bought a relatively new three-bedroom, two-bathroom home in a good location and rented rooms to other students while they lived in it. Because they rented out two of their three rooms, some found themselves cash-positive every month. They were reaping the military house hacking benefits back then and are still profiting from these properties many years later. Rents in Pensacola, where they were stationed, have gone up and their mortgage payments remained the same! In fact, loan principal and interest payments (the largest portions of a mortgage payment) will remain the same for the full thirty years of their loan. So, if rents increase by three percent each year — as they have historically — positive cash flow will also increase.

The main idea behind single-family VA Loan hacking:

- Buy a house with more bedrooms than you need (preferably with the 1% Rule in mind for long-term investment)
- Lease the other rooms to reduce your out-of-pocket mortgage cost. Ideally, the rent collected pays your full mortgage amount.

Here is an example of a somewhat aggressive, but effective approach to the VA Loan single-family house hacking method. Let's use First Lieutenant Jones for our example. Here's the breakdown:

- 1stLt Jones checks into his first CH-53E squadron at MCAS New River, NC.
- He purchases a four-bedroom home for approximately $175,000.
- He pays $1,073 (mortgage) + $80 (utilities) every month: $1,153 total.

- He finds three roommates, one for each extra bedroom. They pay him $500 each: $1,500 total.
- 1stLt Jones pays his mortgage with the rental income and is left with $347 each month in cash flow.
- He then takes the $347 and adds it to his $1,044 in monthly BAH for a total of $1,391.
- Jones thinks he can take it one step further to ensure his strategy works out perfectly, so. . .
- Rather than spend the extra money, he puts that $1,391 toward the principal debt every month.
- After twelve months, this totals $16,692. This amount is *on top of* the $2,758.77 he has paid on the principal, simply by paying his mortgage.

- As a result, in just one year, Jones has paid off $19,450.77 of his loan principal, which is 11.11 percent of his home's total value!
- By this point, 1stLt Jones has been properly educated by ADPI and knows that after he refinances his VA Loan into a conventional loan, he can get a one-time restoration of entitlement, and repeat the process with another VA Loan. Maybe with a larger asset!

After refinancing, since Lieutenant Jones only has 11.11 percent equity in his house, he will have to pay a slightly higher interest rate and might have to pay Primary Mortgage Insurance (PMI). This is common unless you have at least an 80 percent LTV. Remember, this was only twelve months of effort and does not account for potential appreciation. If the house also appreciated in value (either market or forced appreciation through rehab or small improvements) he might already have accrued 20 percent equity in total. But either way, paying PMI does not bother him because he knows that putting in any additional cash he's saved over the last year would hurt his reserve savings. He is relatively conservative financially and understands the power of leverage. Jones, the now real estate investor-savvy guy that he is, would rather use that money for rehabbing his next home or save it for another investment that would produce more in monthly income down the road.

He is motivated by his success, keeps the momentum moving, and takes the next step. Since he now has his VA Loan eligibility back after his one-time restoration, he decides to move and purchase a similar house using a similar strategy.

His options are as follows:

Move locally with the same tenants

- His tenants move with him, and he might offer to pay for their moving expenses.
- He would then find a good property manager to manage and find new tenants for his first house.
- Now his first property has become an almost completely hands-off, cash flowing rental property.

Leave the tenants in place

- He leaves his current tenants in his first house if they don't want to move
- A property manager fills his vacancy with a new tenant and provides a new lease with all remaining tenants.
- Jones finds new tenants for the new house he will house hack. Again, he can find two or three people he already knows to fill the new property.

At the end of his four years in North Carolina:

- Jones will have two cash flowing assets growing his net worth every month, which will slowly increase due to annual rent increases and appreciation.
- He will own about 10 to 15 percent equity in two properties for a grand total of about $100,000 (that he did not invest any money into, by the way).
- He will make positive cash flow from each house. Jones uses these extra income streams to enhance his comfort of living and lifestyle or to keep buying more assets.

It is clear why this military house hacking strategy is the most popular for those getting started; it's simple to understand and easy to implement.

Small Multifamily Hacking with VA Loan or FHA/203K Loan

This method is perfect for those who already have a spouse, family, or simply do not want anyone living in their spare bedrooms. It allows you to buy a decent home wherever you are stationed with 0 percent down payment with a VA Loan or small down payment with an FHA loan.

Note: An FHA loan is a product in which you can put as little as 3.5 percent down payment, must typically have at least a 580 credit score, and will need to pay PMI.

Each tenant will live in their own unit, providing more privacy.

Main concept:

- Buy a two-, three-, or four-unit complex, mimicking the example above.
- Rent out the units you are not living in. The rent from the other tenants will replace most of your mortgage payment for the entire building (ideally, the combined rents are equal to or greater than your PITI-PMMV expenses).
- As you live in one unit, you can slowly force appreciation by completing some small upgrades that are common for your unit type, size, and location. Sometimes that is just a fresh coat of paint and new carpet, while other markets might benefit from granite countertops and stainless appliances. Then, when you are finished and a tenant moves out of an adjacent unit, you could move to their unit (next door) and repeat the process. Eventually, you will have slowly renovated each unit, increasing the entire building's rental income potential.

Note: Eligible service members can use the VA Loan to buy up to a four-unit, owner-occupied residential property. There are circumstances where an existing commercial unit can also be included. Additionally, there are some dual-military (married couple, both service members) advantages. Consult your VA lender for details.

To this point, Jones has used his first VA Loan, refinanced it to a conventional loan, and used his one-time restoration to buy another asset. Understanding and seeing how impactful investing in real estate can be, he decides to do a little more research prior to checking in to his squadron at MCAS New River.

When he prepares to PCS, he connects with an ADPI lender and realizes that his current home does not have enough equity for a conventional loan refinance. Therefore, his best option at the new duty station is likely to use an FHA loan to buy the next property. Because of his cash flow from his properties, he has saved between $15,000 to $20,000 while at flight school, which is exactly what he needs for his FHA loan down payment.

After working with his ADPI lender and real estate agent, he made an offer on a four-unit complex near Sneads Ferry, NC, and closed on the deal forty-five days later for $460,000.

The property already had three of the four units leased to tenants, so Jones simply moved into the fourth unit. Here is how it worked out for him:

- Jones's mortgage was just under $2,650 every month.
- The tenants paid $900 a month for rent and a flat $50 utility fee. This added up to $2,850 a month and easily covered Jones's mortgage payment — including PMI.

- He saved all his BAH and after twelve months had enough equity to refinance the property and buy another multifamily complex with another FHA (or VA, depending) loan.
- Jones handed his first four-unit property off to a good property manager and pays them for their services.
- With all four units leased he makes approximately $600 in cash flow per month.
- He is also gaining about $500-$600 a month in equity for the first several years (this number is rising every month as principal decreases).

Throughout his career, in alignment with VA and lender guidelines, and with his goals and creativity in mind, Jones can repeat this process.

Short Term/Vacation Rentals

Vacation rentals can be a great way to house hack. Popular businesses in this space, like VRBO® and Airbnb®, have taken the vacation rental market by storm and have given hotels a run for their money. Because these models don't require companies to build tall buildings in desirable places, this modern house hack gives the homeowner (or investor) the ability to transform the empty space in their home into a money-making machine.

To succeed with this type of hack, all it really takes is some vision, structure, and a little creativity to get things going well. If you are considering using vacation rentals to house hack, make sure you research your local rules, ordinances, laws, and CC&R and HOA restrictions. You will also want to talk with other investors who have been using this strategy in your local market. If you are uncertain about how to check other vacation rental listings and get in touch with another owner, or how to find an investor, just go to a local real estate meetup and ask.

Once you are certain you want to use this potentially lucrative house hacking method, proceed with the steps below.

Step 1: Have a Vision

First, you must determine which features of your home-turned-investment may be attractive to prospective short-term tenants.

Consider the following questions:

- What type of tenants do you intend to attract? Business people? Vacation-goers? Military families?
- What features about the house (location, amenities, price) may attract that tenant or the desired duration of stay?
- How many rooms do you intend to rent? The whole property or just a portion?
- Will you rent it only during the summer or winter (short-term)? Or can you rent it to tenants throughout the year (long-term, multiple tenants)?
- How profitable can this become vs. the amount of work you will need to put in (turnover, cleaning costs, damage, etc.)?

74

- Are you renting an entire house or just a room or two?
- What does the business plan look like if you are deployed or at a training?

These are just some the basic questions you need to answer before you list your home on a vacation rental site. The strategy you put together sets the foundation for what you do next. If you decide to live in the home while you rent it, you'll be limited to renting out any extra space you have in the home. This could potentially be a loft, a spare bedroom, or even just a sofa. With Airbnb for instance, whatever extra space you have available to rent in your home will suffice. If you decide to rent your entire place, either while on deployment or if you have an extra unit on your property, you will have more options for *how* you rent and to whom you choose to rent.

The location of the property can make a difference in the crowd that it attracts. If your property is by the beach, you might expect to draw families or large groups. If your rental is in the heart of downtown in a major city, you might expect a younger crowd or tourists that want to explore the area. So, make sure you have thought this through before you begin to decorate, take pictures, and actively advertise.

Knowing how often and the time of year you want to rent the property to transient occupants is another critical point in mapping out your vision. If you are looking to rent the property seasonally, when you are on deployment, temporary duty for a military school, or all year, you will need to make sure your listing accurately reflects your intentions. You will need to know exactly what dates are available and that the price will be per night.

Action Items:

- Decide if you want to rent your entire home, a spare unit, or just a portion of your home.
- Do research on local attractions near you. List five things people may want to see and do locally and include the activities in the listing.
- Think about the types of tenants your property will attract. Identify three groups of people that may want to rent your property. List five things to incorporate into your rental that may entice each group.

Step 2: Structure the Business

Once you have decided who your target market is and how you want to rent your property, it's time to start setting things up. The first things you need to put into place are a company or group of people to call to fix problems (this might be a property manager if you need one), maybe a handyman, and a system or protocol for how you want to operate. Having a Standard Operating Procedure (SOP) checklist will allow you to automate a lot of what you will be expected to do for each tenant and/or property.

If you are still active duty, one of the likely challenges you will run into with an active vacation rental is having limited to no communication when you are on duty, training, deployed, or at sea. For this reason, an SOP and a trustworthy friend, partner, or spouse could be of great benefit. He or she can run all the operations of the business while you are fulfilling your obligations to your job. Their responsibilities could include communicating with the tenants, scheduling bookings, handling the activity logs, calling service professionals to fix problems, and making sure the property is clean during tenant turnover. Whoever this makeshift property manager is, it is important for them to be organized, responsible, and good at customer service. Even if you only expect to be gone for a short period of time, consider having this person on standby. Another option would be to hire a company to act as a professional short-term rental property manager.

In this business, as you may discover, it only takes one bad review to have a very negative effect on your rental. So, make sure you cover your six and have the right people in place to handle the job. Whether that is a professional property manager or a responsible friend, be prepared.

If you are handy with repairs around the home, you can save yourself some serious money. With a high volume of tenants rotating through your property, there are bound to be a few mishaps, damaged or lost items, plumbing issues, and more. If you are not much of a do-it-yourselfer, you should start looking at service professionals in your area prior to advertising the rental—there may be local Airbnb management companies that offer a full range of services for your business. Consider these companies as they will be a one-stop-shop for everything you need. If you do find the need for professional management, just make sure you factor that into the rent to cover your bases.

Here are some must-have service providers if you choose to manage the property yourself:

- Plumber
- Electrician
- Handyman
- Cleaning Service

Note: You can always charge a cleaning fee to your tenants to recoup the costs of turnover, which is very common. In case of major repairs, you can withhold a portion of their security deposit for things that go beyond normal wear and tear. Just ensure that is included in the contract.

Once you have your management and maintenance teams in place, you'll want to create a system. How are you going to operate your rental? What is the minimum number of nights you will require guests to book? How many days in advance will you want them to book? How many days will they have to cancel without penalty? How many days will you reserve between tenants? These are some of the questions you'll need to have answers to before you start operating. As you answer them, think about how tying in maintenance and cleaning will work. What if your cleaning team is not available? Do you have a backup team? In addition, come up with a process for an emergency. How or who will you call? How will the situation be handled? Talking to other investors who have done vacation rentals in your community can be helpful and may give you insight you would not have otherwise considered.

Action Items:

- Talk to at least three people that operate vacation rentals in your area. You can find them by going to a host site (such as AirBnb) and simply sending them a message asking their advice on how to handle maintenance, management, and tenant turnover.
- Decide whether you are going to manage the property yourself or hire some help.
- Find good service professionals in the area and communicate with them on how you wish to run your business. You can ask for discounts with continued use of their services. Find backup crews in case of emergency.

Step 3: Be Creative

Now that you have your structure in place, it is time to get to the fun part: turn your vision into a reality. Use your creativity and find some good furnishings, decorations, and amenities to make your listing the best it can be. Remember, you want to highlight the features and benefits that you wrote down in Step 1. If you struggle in the creativity department, it can be helpful to refer to HGTV or Pinterest.

When furnishing your home, you can save money by shopping at sites like OfferUp, Craigslist, or take a trip to Home Goods or a thrift store. You should *never* overpay for your furnishings due to the amount of wear and tear they are going to receive from your tenants. Your household items will wear at a faster rate, so keep that in mind as you shop.

Look for furnishings that will best match what you want your rental to look like. If you are into refurbishing old furniture (or if shabby chic is your thing) the thrift shop or a flea market may be the perfect place for you to go shopping. Always see if you can haggle down prices to save a few more dollars and boost your return on investment. You would be surprised at how much you can save just by asking.

Don't hold back on filling your property up with important amenities. Refer to your vision and think about what your target market will want to see. Do you have spices in your kitchen? Do you have extra linens? Do you offer soap, razors, or feminine products? What about good Wi-Fi? Today, having Wi-Fi is an absolute must, unless your listing is in the middle of nowhere and you are purposely advertising it as an opportunity to get off the grid.

It is beneficial to fill your property with important provisions that a non-vacation rental might have. If you live on a beach or lake, it may be a good idea to provide flotation devices or water sports toys. Is there toilet paper in the restrooms? You want your tenants to say, "They thought of everything!" There is a strong likelihood the tenant will forget something, so when they see you have it on hand, you will have exceeded their expectations. This is how you get great reviews and repeat business.

Once you have your place looking like an HGTV model home, you're ready for a photographer to come and bring it to life. You would be amazed how professionals can make a place look by the proper placement of photos. If you have a good camera, the photos should be well lit and full of color. If your kitchen or bathroom are white, be sure to add a few items that are bright and vibrant to make the listing pop. Most people choose vacation rentals over hotels because they like the warm feeling of being home, so make sure your pictures capture that your vacation rental is warm and inviting. And don't forget to turn on all the lights!

Action Items:

- Make a list of all the essential items you will need for your rental. Look at stores like Costco, Sam's Club or Walmart to save on buying smaller items in bulk (toothpaste, shampoo, tissues, etc.)

- Look online or at "economy" stores for discounted items or furniture other people are selling. Craigslist, thrift stores, and the like.
- Hire a photographer to take quality photos of your place when you are done decorating.

Note: Make sure to have safety items in the property, to include: fire extinguishers, smoke detectors, carbon monoxide sensors, etc.

Step 4: Listing the Short-Term Rental

Advertising your property is the fourth and final step. This is surprisingly easier than you think, just follow the steps on the website of your choice to make the process a bit smoother. Sites like Airbnb.com or VRBO.com will run you through their process by the numbers. Three of the most important things you'll want to spend time on to catch the eye of a potential tenant, are as follows: your cover photo, the amount you'll charge per night, and the minimum number of nights your tenants can book.

Choosing the right cover photo is crucial because the cover photo is one of the first things your customers will see. You want something that will attract your target tenant to click on your listing. It is important to make sure that photo is either bright, vibrant, or has some curious or quirky features. Good pictures to use are landscapes, artwork, key features (like a pool) or surrounding attractions in the area.

The next thing people will see, almost simultaneously with the photo, is your listing price. This is also important to get right. The best way to make sure you are not over-charging is to look at comparable vacation rentals in your area. Run a search to see what others are charging for a similar listing. You will want to consider the number of beds, whether it is a listing for a single room or for a whole house and maybe even what amenities are offered.

You should ensure the price accurately reflects what is expected in your area, but also understand that price can dictate the quality of tenants you receive. Common wisdom tells us the less money people spend on things, the less value they will place on it and perhaps the less they will care for it. Therefore, be sure not to undervalue your rental or the service you are providing.

One of the most critical steps in your listing is the process by which your tenants will complete their bookings. Convenience will drive momentum as your listing continues to gain traction and inquiries start to come in more frequently. You need to decide whether your guests can book automatically or if they need to contact you first. Most websites will require guests to have two forms of identification and to initiate a qualification process to confirm bookings automatically. Therefore, if you trust the system, allowing tenants to book your listing automatically will increase the speed of your bookings. Automatic verification is not a bad move if you are trying to maximize as many bookings as possible. If you are trying to regulate thoroughly who comes into your property, stick to vetting all the potential tenants personally. This way, you will be able to get to know the tenants before they book the property.

Action Items:

- Choose the best cover photo to entice prospective tenants to view your listing over others.
- Analyze the listings in your area that best compare to your home. Determine a competitive price range that will work for your listing.
- Decide if you want people to book automatically or if you want to vet every tenant as they book.

At this point, you are ready to go! Make sure you track your renters and keep a cool head when things don't go 100 percent according to plan. If you manage your expectations and understand that you may learn more and profit less from your first experience, you will be pleasantly surprised with how things turn out.

Other Value-add Hacks

So far, we have unearthed some valuable house hacking tools to use for your typical single-family and small multifamily units. Some of these are well-known to people with real estate investing experience and some are unique to you, the veteran or active-duty service member.

You will read about other testimonials later in this book, but first, here are some value-add hacks that can be a game-changer to the bottom line — something few people think of when getting started.

First, consider a scenario in which a soldier used a VA Loan (again, zero down) to buy a fourplex near his installation. The two-story property is situated on a semi-busy street on one acre and the building is otherwise surrounded by grass. This type of property, size of lot, and location was specifically sought out by the service member using a vetted, educated, military lender, and real estate agent.

Here are some additional potential streams of income that this soldier applied to his Military House Hack to increase his monthly revenue:

- **Dog park:** If there is a small area that can be enclosed inexpensively with chain-link fencing, this amenity could encourage pet owners to rent from you.
- **Pet rent:** Many tenants will gladly pay a non-refundable pet deposit (for example, $350) and a monthly pet rent. Depending on your area, that could be an extra $15-$50/month.
- **Cell tower leases**: This might be a stretch but call your local cell service providers and ask if there is demand for leasing a portion of your land for a new cell tower.
- **Covered/Reserved parking:** You can rent out a garage or covered parking or if you own the lot, paint a

designated/reserved spot for a tenant who is willing to pay monthly.

- **Ratio Utility Billing Service (RUBS):** This is starting to dive a little more into the commercial multifamily realm, but if you are paying water, sewer, electric and/or gas bills as an owner, you could use this system to bill back the other tenants. Your local market will dictate whether tenants will pay this or not, so call your property manager or do some research to see if this is a viable option.

- **Storage:** You have plenty of land in this scenario, so either build a shed or go to Home Depot, buy an 8-by-10 shed, section it off inside and rent out each area to tenants for storage. If you have a basement, you can portion it off as well.

- **Laundry machines:** If you have a laundry room, there are companies that will provide laundry machines and split the proceeds with you. Or you can provide in-unit machines for an extra fee.

- **Vending machines:** If there is a safe, sheltered breezeway and an outlet you could make some extra money by installing vending machines. There are even gumball/non-perishable candy machine companies (no power required) that will split profits.

- **Trash valet:** This sounds ridiculous, but if you have a tenant who needs this service, you can offer to pick up their garbage from outside their door for a reasonable weekly or monthly fee.

- **Play structure/BBQ** A playground is another amenity to attract tenants and charge (potentially) higher rent. *Note: You will need to ensure you have adequate insurance for these structures.*

- **Simple tech package:** This is a small convenience, but for $25 or so you can install a USB outlet in the kitchen and/or other rooms. Tenants may even want touch-key door locks if it is offered. You can charge $5-$10/month for this.

- **Renter's insurance:** There are companies that will offer a revenue share if you get your tenants to use their insurance.
- **Billboards**: One example where this could work is if you have a rental with some land on a back-road highway on the way to a nearby military installation. You could build a couple small makeshift billboards and spray paint "Your Ad Here" with a phone number. Fifty dollars per month per sign can add up and it also helps the advertiser!
- **Solar hacking**: The premise is simple: generate excess solar power and sell it back to your electric company. You likely will want to purchase a property that already has solar installed (not leased). These systems are not cheap, so the numbers would have to work for you, both short- and long-term.

There are dozens of amenities, upgrades, or services an owner can offer to increase his net operating income. This short list shows the multitude of value-add strategies you could employ if you are creative with all your property has to offer and aware of local trends and the needs of your tenants.

Military House Hacking:
Real-Life Examples

Tim Kelly's Story

After purchasing my first primary residence back in 2011, I became more and more interested in real estate investing. I knew there were many ways someone could make money with real estate, but I had no idea where to begin.

It all started by thinking it was cool that I could personally renovate my own house with some basic upgrades and then be rewarded by its value increasing. Real estate investors call this adding "sweat equity" or more formally, "forced appreciation."

My growing interest in real estate investing and personal finance led me to become a Navy Command Financial Specialist (CFS). I loved being a CFS because of the continual opportunity to learn more about money and wealth and help other service members improve their financial situation.

My first ah-ha moment came once I discovered the world of podcasts. *BiggerPockets* and a few other great shows added immeasurable value to my personal journey.

As many real estate investors will admit, a wonderful little purple book is what really pushed them into taking a massive leap toward real estate investing. I stumbled across *Rich Dad Poor Dad* by Robert Kiyosaki, and it consumed me. My interest in real estate and building wealth exploded! I never looked back.

House Hack #1 - Accidental House Hack

I used my VA Loan to close on my first primary home in 2011. The home was in a great neighborhood and was in a growing part of town with constant development and gentrification. The house was unique because it had two master bedrooms. One was on the second level, where my wife and I slept, and one was on the lower level where we anticipated our family would stay when they came to visit.

The extra space in the home, coupled with my passion for real estate and finance, sparked the idea of simply renting out the lower level to a trusted individual who was looking for a rental in that area. We found a great roommate and the timing could not have been better. I was deployed early that year, so my wife enjoyed having company around, plus they helped pay more than half the mortgage payment!

It is funny looking back today because we house hacked without even realizing it. I simply thought I bought a house that was too big, but it turned out to be a great introduction to house hacking. In fact, I was experiencing the power of real estate investing first-hand.

After our first roommate had moved on, we had no problems finding someone to move in immediately, mostly due to the nice area and perfect size of the room we were renting. So, there we were, hooked!

House Hack #2 - Fourplex Using an FHA 203k Loan!

Soon after our first house hack, and after diving headfirst into real estate investment education, books, and more podcasts, I learned about the 203k Loan. This is an FHA-backed loan that allows you to "wrap" (include) rehab costs into the price of the home, only requires a 3.5 percent down payment, and can be used on any property from one to four units. The only catch is that *you* must occupy one of the units.

This is considered an owner-occupied loan (like the VA Loan), whereas the borrower must have the intent to move into the house or one of the units for at least six months and one day (according to the lender).

We were able to find a fourplex to execute this new strategy and I must tell you, we were excited!

Here are the rough numbers:

- Purchase price = $145,000
- Rehab budget = $100,000
- Down payment = $15,000
- Total loan amount = $230,000

Originally, the rehab was scheduled to take no more than ninety days. I was surprised that the bank and the general contractors agreed to the renovation plan and timeline, especially with $100,000 of work to be done! But they agreed, we closed on time, and I was scheduled to move in shortly after.

Since the rehab would take some time, and I had recently PCSed from another state, I had to find a short-term rental in the area. Yes, I had to pay rent where I was living, as well as the mortgage on the fourplex. Yes, I needed to have liquid capital to make this possible. But getting four completely renovated units for $15,000 was well worth the effort!

In the end, because of some permitting issues and construction delays, the rehab ended up taking eight months and I never actually got to move into this new fourplex hack. Eventually, my wife and I realized that we were happy where we lived during those eight months of renovations, so we decided to stay put and to rent out the last of the four units, which we had initially intended on moving into.

It is now a very nice cash-flowing fourplex and I will look to refinancing it into a commercial investment loan very soon.

House Hack #3 - Triplex with a VA Rehab Loan

Believe it or not, there are banks out there that offer a VA Rehab Loan. This means your 0 percent down payment will cover both a house and all the renovation costs! What?!

This is an amazing benefit to those who have served and if you are even considering getting involved in the real estate game, this opportunity really begs the question: Why not?

Even with a family, there are plenty of small multifamily properties that are nice, two- or three-bedroom units that will be compatible with family living. Even better, you may find separate, detached dwellings so you will not have to share walls, which seems to be one of the biggest turn-offs for individuals thinking about doing this.

In this situation, I was able to find a perfect single-family home for my family in one of the most desirable neighborhoods, the best school district, and with a completely detached duplex in the back! Moreover, it sits on a large corner lot, so the house and the duplex are facing different streets. No one would ever know the owner of the home also owns the duplex! It's a great set-up.

Again, this was a 0 percent down payment VA Loan, and I was able to wrap in $70,000 of renovation costs as part of the deal. I did, however, need to bring about $6,000 to close, but again, well worth it.

As it stands now, I'm really looking forward to completing the rehab on all three units so I can rent out each duplex unit for $850-$950 and basically live for free. That's *really* house hacking at its best. It's a great feeling knowing that the home I'm living in is not a major financial liability like it is for many other people I know.

The beautiful thing about hacking your housing is that it puts you at an incredible advantage to take your real estate business to the next level. Not only will you become a homeowner, an investor, and a landlord, but you'll also be able to get paid to live and literally stack up capital at an accelerated pace! This, in turn, will quickly put you in the position to grow your buy-and-hold rental portfolio.

Key takeaways:

- When you house hack, you can become a homeowner, investor, landlord, and a property manager all in one deal! Like a VA Loan, you must intend to occupy the property when using a 203K Loan — and it can get you in trouble if you do not.
- You must have a solid financial foundation established before you can begin this journey. I cannot stress this enough.
- You must have a support system and a team of people who have your back. As it turns out, Active Duty Passive Income can provide the financial education, support, and services you need to reach your goals.

Eric Upchurch's Story

I will preface my story by saying that my life's purpose and passion is not to be rich. On the contrary, it is to educate, empower, and help people grow. This is what drives me. It's the reason I chose to become an enlisted soldier after attending college (starting as an E-4 instead of an O-1). What I have discovered through the Active Duty Passive Income community is that I get to combine two of my passions — real estate and mentorship — to fulfill that mission.

"Ah ha!," I shouted to myself when I had the most enlightening and powerful thought of my life: I was going to get rich . . . slowly but surely.

In fact, I've had two similar moments that affected me so profoundly that I was sure I would succeed — OK, so maybe one of them was the result of too much coffee one morning, but that doesn't change the impact of that moment for me.

I hope that in reading this book and getting involved with the Active Duty Passive Income community, you, too, will experience *your* epiphany — whatever it takes for you to get started. Because if I did it, you can too.

Epiphany Moment #1:

There I was in late 2014, listening to the audio version of *Rich Dad, Poor Dad* in my truck just prior to attending one of those "guru" single-family house flipping seminars you always hear about. In preparation for the event, I was listening to the book hoping to hit the ground running in a ballroom full of professional investors. I had heard from someone that it was a good read, so I thought, *What the heck, why not?* (I have to say, now I love *Rich Dad, Poor Dad* and recommend it for anyone — period. It doesn't matter if real estate is your thing or not.) I found myself immersed in the story and halfway through the book I wanted to *be* Rich

93

Dad. I thought: *He makes it sound so simple. I can do that!* And off I went to my first real estate training event that I was certain would launch my future success.

Epiphany Moment #2:

This was the too-much-coffee moment. Nevertheless, it represented an important mindset shift.

After the house-flipping seminar, I moved on from merely dreaming about flipping houses in the San Francisco Bay Area to reading a string of mindset books to get my mind into an entrepreneurial focus. I wanted to start taking action, but knew I needed a solid foundation first. I read *Think and Grow Rich* by Napoleon Hill and *The Millionaire Mind* by Thomas J. Stanley. About three quarters through Millionaire Mind, I had this moment that just kind of hit me like a ton of bricks: I am going to be a millionaire! I then found myself loudly repeating, as prompted by the author, "I have a millionaire mind! I have a millionaire mind!" That may sound cheesy, and it certainly felt as much, but at that moment, there were *no* limitations on my mind.

More importantly, this is where I decided I no longer cared what anyone else says or thinks about my future: it's not *their* future, it's *mine*! I will succeed in real estate. It was decided.

My Personal Version of the Military House Hack

If you are an active-duty soldier, sailor, airman, marine, coast guardsman, space cadet, or veteran, you have one big advantage over everyone else in the world: you may not have money to invest in real estate yet, but you have one absolutely *amazing* capital-building tool through the power of the VA Loan.

When I was stationed at Hunter Army Airfield in Savannah, Georgia, we purchased a new construction single-family home for around $150,000. My wife and I bought it while I was on my first rotation to Iraq in 2006. Initially, we were nervous about out-of-pocket expenses, but ultimately, we were able to use my first VA Loan eligibility, put zero down, and even roll the VA funding fee (2 percent) and closing costs into the loan.

That property ended up becoming a rental from 2010 until 2018 when I sold it for a profit. I'll also mention that since I put zero dollars into it, every dollar I made each month from it over the eight years was technically an *infinite* return (any return/zero invested = infinite return). The idea that you can own an asset producing cash each month, year after year, and have NO MONEY in the deal was very exciting.

In early 2011, I left a career in 160th Special Operations Aviation Regiment and headed back to the San Francisco Bay Area for a job that paid just enough to get by but was near my wife's family. It was a great company and a good opportunity for me to transition smoothly from the army to civilian life, but I had no idea how expensive the Bay Area was going to be!

Fast forward two years: we had been renting a house and saving money when my wife got pregnant with our second son. Since we were following the Dave Ramsey mentality the previous two years and were completely out of debt, we were now ready to enter the expensive Bay Area real estate market. Well, we thought we were ready. We were thankful to have a solid financial foundation, which made all the difference.

After attending the previously mentioned flipping bootcamp (and subsequent advanced course upsell), I knew how to proceed. However, since I was not yet poised to flip houses in the Bay Area, I had to think of a way to start investing given my specific circumstances. That was the one thing I consistently recognized as most important: taking action.

Here are the three strategies, in chronological order, that began our five-year journey of hacking our way to success with the VA Loan. But, before you continue, let me preface the explanation of my experiences by stating what you will inevitably be thinking: Well, 2012 was a good time to buy real estate. It sure was. But for those of you who read this and say, "Well you caught the market at the right time," we may be headed toward similar times. By reading below and learning now, you are taking the next steps toward being ready yourself!

My recommendation is to act now. Get educated and execute your strategy when the time is good for you. I know there will be market downturns to come. I'm expecting it, I'm ready for it, and I'm excited about it. You should be, too, especially if you are or were a member of the US Armed Forces.

First Hack: VA Loan, All Market Appreciation (Two-plus Years' Ownership)

In late 2012 we bought the first home. Notice I called it a home, not a house or property, as one would normally say for an investment. We had originally intended to stay in this home. It was a beautiful, newer, four-bedroom, three-bathroom duet (an attached two-story property, like a townhouse-duplex). It also happened to be a short sale, where the owner had been relocated to Texas for work and the previous buyer had fallen through. The house was listed at a price we could barely afford even though it was almost the cheapest home on the market. But we knew the market

96

was appreciating and it was in a great neighborhood with good schools.

For a kid from Iowa, who'd only used a VA Loan to buy that relatively inexpensive house in Georgia so far, I had major, major sticker shock! Do construction materials cost five times more in California? The cool part about this property is that it was in great shape, had all the original builder upgrades, and needed no work at all. So, we got preapproved for a VA Loan and offered full asking price the same day we saw it. Now here's where it gets good. Since there were almost no comps for a duet built in 2008, we ended up getting the home for what it appraised for, which was $50K *less* than our offer!

In 2014, after owning this property for two years—and after just starting to learn about how to invest in real estate—we contacted an agent to see what it was now worth. To our surprise, it had appreciated 36 percent! And since we owned the property more than two years, if we sold it, we would pay NO tax on any net gains. You can do the math, but that was one heck of a great investment. The point is not to call this strategy a hack, but more to note that without the VA Loan, I never would have been able to enter the Bay Area real estate market. Additionally, you must be creative, no matter your strategy.

We now had a good bit of money for a down payment on our next home, but my point of view on real estate had changed forever.

Second Hack: Conventional Loan, All Forced Appreciation (Less Than One Year Ownership)

While in the process of selling the first house, we took our kids tide-pooling in the Northern Monterey Bay area one day when we stumbled across an open house in a nearby little beach town. This house was two blocks from a local beach, so the location was great. It was a four-bedroom, two-bathroom property that was outdated, but it had no major issues and we could see that with some TLC it would be a beautiful spot to live. Since my salary had risen at my job, I felt comfortable stretching our finances a bit while using the new-found profits from the last house for the down payment. After all, I was once again *certain* this was our forever dream home.

We put in an offer for the full asking price and it was accepted! Surprised, my wife and I quickly dreamed up plans to make necessary upgrades using some of the profits from the first house, but then two things occurred. First, we realized this house had a weird layout. Second, we had a few conversations with neighbors and found that the neighborhood was slowly starting to turn over into an area of out-of-town retirees who wanted their *retirement* dream home.

"Ah ha! An exit strategy!," I immediately thought. We could keep this type of buyer in mind as we started renovations! I can't say this was a thought my wife had, but I couldn't help myself. I was thinking strategically about real estate now.

With this in mind, we started by removing an odd centrally located bedroom (thus, converting the house into a 3/2), which then opened space that extended the master bathroom by six feet and added four feet of new space in the main living area near the kitchen. Remove a bedroom? Why would anyone ever do that? Seems like it would devalue the property, right? Not for a retiree who wants to live by the beach and only needs three bedrooms!

After about six weeks and roughly $50,000, some sweat, and a lot of trips to Home Depot, the renovation was complete.

We now had a beautiful, large master bathroom and an open floor concept. The kitchen was completely updated with cabinets and quartz counters. The interior was painted with Spanish Sand and Sea Breeze Blue colors to give it a great beach vibe. Outside, I stained the concrete driveway myself, epoxied the garage floor, and installed a cool copper outdoor shower with beautiful tile work that made rinsing off after a day at the beach a breeze.

I'll insert a cool fact here: Remember that flipping seminar I went to? Well, one of the contractors that I met at the event became a good friend and agreed to only charge labor and materials on the renovation! When I applied for permits for the work, the city valued the rehab at $180,000. This goes to show how important networking is. You never know who you will meet!

The valuation on the cost of renovation from the city also made me curious to see what the property was now worth, so I contacted the listing agent from whom we bought the property to see what he thought. Fast forward two weeks: we got a full price, all cash offer from — you guessed it — a retiree from San Diego. There's more to the story, but it felt like a blink of an eye.

In only nine months, the property appreciated 29 percent and sold at a higher price point than the first house. Having owned this property less than one year, we were able to capitalize on forced appreciation (the rehab) alone, but the exit was a little more complicated.

Typically, one would have to pay short-term capital gains tax of close to 34 percent on net profit, but because my employer thought it was best that I move about seventy miles away, I ended up not owing any capital gains tax. Had I needed to, I would have paid the tax and it still would have been an amazing profit.

Note: You should always consult a CPA when complicated tax scenarios arise.

Third Hack: Combination of Forced and Market Appreciation (Exactly 366-day Ownership)

Third time's the charm? We sure hoped so! To be honest, every time we moved into any of these homes, we wanted them to be the one that we would stay in forever. Since I'm handy and always thinking about real estate, they all ended up as live-in flips. I couldn't help it and my wife is a saint! I owe all our success to her. These strategies take a patient, supportive spouse who can see the big picture, is willing to be agile, and embraces adaptation even while raising two kids. The final house on which we used the live-in-flip/hack was a four-bedroom, two-bathroom house with a pool that backed up to a forty-mile-long bike trail and was situated a block away from a high-ranking and very desirable elementary school. We ended up putting $30,000 (again, money that came from both the original VA Loan hack as well as the beach house hack) into superficial upgrades including three new garage doors, all new pool equipment, stained concrete, crown molding, and more. Lots of sweat equity went into this one, and I did almost all the work myself.

I started thinking: Why don't I investigate selling this one myself, so I can save the commission? It's important to constantly think of how you can improve your position. How can you get creative to maximize profit? Solution: for $384, a couple dozen hours of studying, and one state exam, I got my California Real Estate Salesperson license. Did I know what I was doing? Absolutely not. But I wanted to be bold, courageous, and continue to learn. Plus, knew if I represented myself as an agent, selling my own home, the

100

commission I would save on a million-dollar home in the Bay Area was enough to get me over my nerves.

After simply posting the house on Zillow's "Make Me Move" and adding two open house times in one weekend, I found an interested buyer who was not yet represented by an agent. He offered full price, my broker worked up the paperwork, and I ended up saving $70,000 on commissions.

This third house, which had already appreciated by 10 percent, was sold in 366 days. Coincidence? Nope. I knew that at the 366-day mark I would only have to pay long-term capital gains (as opposed to short term). So, by delaying the closing (contractually) until that day, I saved about another 15 percent on what otherwise would have been close to 34 percent tax. Once we closed, I had my CPA calculate what taxes I owed Uncle Sam and I cut a check immediately.

If you are going to try this strategy, you can mitigate some risk by keeping in mind that all these houses had one thing in common: a great location and at least one desirable feature. This always helps with appreciation and attractiveness to sellers and will make your journey a little easier if you keep that in mind.

This part of my investment career is what I refer to as my capital-building phase. Since then, I have expanded my real estate portfolio to include self-directed IRA investments, tax liens, private lending, out-of-state turnkey rentals, two large syndications as a passive investor, and some small multifamily units. I've also purchased over 1,000 apartment and storage units as a active investor with partners.

I'll leave you with this. If you are curious about how to get started in the real estate investing business, I recommend you follow these steps: Learn all you can, network your butt off, add value to others, and take massive action. If you do these four things consistently, with the intention to be only one percent better daily, success will hunt *you* down. And your future self will thank you.

Mike Foster's Story

When it came to financial literacy, like most Americans, I was illiterate. I never had a role model I looked up to financially. I grew up in a poor family in a very low-income community. I had a lot of love, but money was never something we spoke about because it was always a hard conversation. I grew up thinking it was rude and awkward to talk with people about their finances and I was expected to never ask. I liked the idea of having a financially knowledgeable figure in my life, but financial mentorship was not something I thought was possible.

The first four years of my Naval career were spent in Sasebo, Japan, without much of a thought toward my future. When I wasn't busy learning how to be a division officer on one of the smallest and toughest warships in the fleet, I was mostly partying and adventuring in the land of the Rising Sun. But when the time came to PCS, I couldn't stop thinking: What do I do next? What did I accomplish in the last four years?

I am a driven guy, so this first tour left me with a sour taste for the navy. Not because the navy had let me down, but because I had not really focused on personal development at all.

I was struggling with finding any harmonious intersection between personal growth and being a naval officer and I started spending some time thinking about what I would do at my ETS (Expiration of Time in Service). At that same time, even though I knew the likelihood of staying in twenty years was slim, I didn't want any limitations on my second tour before it even started. For that reason alone, I committed to making a change.

I evaluated my personal skills, beliefs, wants, and desires and reflected on where I was financially at the time. After a thorough self-analysis, I discovered I had already accrued a bunch of unnecessary debt, I had zero cash-producing assets, and I had nothing positive to carry forward into my next quarter of life. Yes, I had a good paying job and while I was grateful for that, it was difficult to realize I felt like a slave to my organization. I'm sure some of you can relate. I just felt like I was going nowhere. Or like the term Robert Kiyosaki famously coined, I was "in the rat race" of life.

My epiphany moment came in 2016. I turned to God. I asked him to renew my spirit and show me a way to achieve the happiness I was searching for. Regardless of your religion or beliefs, I think it is important to hold a perspective that places someone or something in higher regard than yourself. Believe in something great.

I prayed for Him to educate me, to put me on the path I needed to take in life, and to open my eyes to opportunities I didn't see before. Since I didn't really feel like the military was my calling, I felt I needed some external enlightenment. Slowly but surely, He did just that. If you are struggling as I was, I hope you can find the same clarity and direction because it changed my life.

The first discovery that led me to where I am today was podcasts! I knew that podcasts were a thing while I was in Japan because I used to listen to a DJ on a radio station that talked about them all the time. However, I didn't know they were also for information-gathering. It completely blew my mind when I found people were sharing new ideas, data, and stories from all over the world, from different walks of life, spreading all kinds of information. With this newfound love of learning through podcasts, I was ready to soak up all the info I could! I was hooked. As I write this, I should add that we started the Active Duty Passive Income podcast in 2018.

The next God-given gift that pushed me along in my journey was learning to network. He introduced people into my life that would become a catalyst for my personal growth. Networking and getting to know and work with other like-minded people, may be the most important part of real estate investing. So far it had gotten me focused, inspired, and opened me up to a world of education and opportunity.

I started getting into the business and investment mindset through a friend who introduced me to a Multi-Level Marketing (MLM) company. She then connected me with someone who, even though I have since given up the MLM strategy, is still a mentor to me today. This mentor then introduced me to educational audiobooks and motivational speakers.

Up to this point in life, the concept of sitting down to read a book had never appealed to me. With podcasts and audiobooks, I could now "read" while I was working out, driving, or working on the ship. Motivational speakers were awesome because they were the boost I needed to improve my mood on a bad day. With this new source of knowledge, I started becoming aware of who I was, what I wanted, and what action steps I was or could be taking. Success followed.

Somewhere along the line, my mentor mentioned a book called *Rich Dad, Poor Dad* by Robert Kiyosaki. Because I was just getting started with audiobooks, I put it aside and marked it as just another book to read when I get around to it. This book would eventually change the course of my life.

Months later, while on a team call, I heard one of my commanders say something to the effect of, "don't let your past define who you are, use the models that are out there, then make your own story." He then mentioned *Rich Dad, Poor Dad* as a great book to help shift and open my mindset. His impromptu speech got me thinking about my life, aspirations, ambitions, and which direction I was headed. And it was now the second time I'd heard a recommendation to read this book.

So, I finally read it—if you haven't, add it to your queue immediately after finishing this book. The lessons I learned from *Rich Dad, Poor Dad*, like thousands of other investors and entrepreneurs, opened my eyes to the power of real estate and changed my life forever.

Fast forward six months from that date and I purchased my first real estate investment. After reading audiobooks and listening to podcasts, I knew I needed to act if I wanted to experience the most growth and learning in the real estate industry. I also knew that having a place to live *and* a place to rent out was the way to start.

After some searching, I found a double condo on the beach in Norfolk, Virginia, that I felt would be a good start. Using a creative strategy that I had learned through the podcasts and books I'd read, I negotiated with the seller and bought the top half of the building with a lease-option to buy the bottom half. The seller helped me find someone to sublease the bottom and later, when my wife PCSed to Virginia, we bought the bottom as well!

The summer of our first year as investors, we put the upper condo on Airbnb and it did very well. We made enough money to pay our mortgage for the full year! We then used the surplus income in combination with our wedding gift money to buy two additional investment properties.

One year later, in only our second year of investing in real estate, we had almost doubled our profits. We then reinvested profits to buy a few more in the United States, as well as our first foreign real estate investment while I was deployed. You can see from my experience how a little education, understanding, networking, and creativity can really snowball into something great.

As I type this, I just negotiated a seller-financed deal on an eight-unit property next door that I plan to Airbnb. All of this is happening because I was willing to be comfortable being uncomfortable.

Final Thoughts:

We live in an age where information is not as limited as it was in the past. You truly can change the course of your life if you have the hunger and the desire to find out what is out there. You can produce massive results if you have the determination to put in the work and are willing to sacrifice superficial desires to accomplish your dreams.

You can find the answers you need—or at least your own epiphany moment—in our Military Real Estate Investing Academy™, Action Takers Only Mastermind™ (ATOM) and community, or in books and podcasts just like I did. But it is time to stop watching other people live their best lives. Learn from them, get involved, and live your best life too!

Remember that knowledge is power, but action is authority. Life is not like a narrow channel. There is no easy path and there will always be obstacles to overcome, which is why it is important to surround yourself with like-minded people. We are all in this together. That is why we do what we do for the ADPI community.

Most importantly, along this journey I have met some awesome people and shared great experiences. Real estate investing has brought immense happiness to my life, and I am excited for the opportunity to bring happiness to other people. That's YOU!

"On the strength of one link in the cable, dependeth the might of the chain. Who knows when thou mayest be tested, so live that thou bearest the strain." - Fifth Law of the US Navy

Adam La Barr's Story

My beautiful wife, Raquel, introduced me to the world of real estate investing through her family. My in-laws owned their home free and clear, and they also owned a rental property. It was paid off and producing significant income. This planted a seed and opened my eyes to the real estate world.

Eventually, I dove into real estate education by absorbing every piece of literature, audiobook, or podcast I could find. As mentioned for others in this book, *Rich Dad, Poor Dad* was an amazingly motivating and inspirational book for me. I learned what an asset and a liability are, I learned where I wanted to focus my energy, and I learned my in-laws were making some sense! It took time, but I discovered my own financial freedom number and began to understand what it would take to not have to rely on a military retirement. That number meant a lot to me because I was injured and unsure of where my military career would take me. I did not know if I would get medically boarded, medically retired, or incur further injuries. I needed to get my family to a point where it did not matter what happened. I was determined to truly understand what my purpose was because that's what drives you through the challenges in life. Focusing on "why" you want to do this will make all the difference in the world. My family is my "why."

After a lot of research, I determined that my strategy was not going to be buying single-family rental houses. While that works well for many people and it is a viable option, I was ambitious and wanted to speed up the process to reach my financial freedom number. I skipped right over single-family and small multifamily investing and went straight into apartment investing. My wife and I knew that we needed to set ourselves up for success and be smart with our money. So, we saved as much money as we could to be prepared to make the right decisions when the opportunity arose.

A strong point must be made before I continue: I started buying properties while stationed overseas. If I can manage to invest in apartments while on active duty and traveling all around the world, anyone can.

"Raquel, I am going to fly out to Los Angeles to go to a conference and meet some people," I proclaimed. I was overseas at the time, so this was not just a quick, cheap flight. I was committed to taking steps toward my goals and I wanted results badly. Thankfully, I have an incredibly supportive wife who knew I had the best interest of my family in mind.

The best part of the trip was the amazing people I met. It was so cool to meet so many like-minded real estate enthusiasts. Many were less educated than me, but because they were just as motivated, we were rubbing elbows with experienced investors and making deals happen. I met some great people, but also found myself helping and teaching almost everyone I encountered. This gave me confidence. I realized I really absorbed a lot of what I researched but I knew I had not yet put it to use. It was time to jump in and take further steps toward my goals. It was time to take *massive action!*

I left Los Angeles more motivated than ever. I sent letters, hired virtual assistants, called more brokers, created partnerships, and continued my education. I entered a multifamily education program, I became an active participant in a mastermind group, and I got a highly experienced mentor. It is not an exaggeration when I say I analyzed probably more than a thousand deals. Why did all this matter? These relationships are what sparked the first couple investments I made. The networking was more important than almost all the previous education I received, and I knew that fostering these relationships was going to pay off.

After several anxious months, I closed on my first deal, a 62-unit apartment! The relationships I built in Los Angeles and through my mastermind group are what put together the partnership for this deal. We purchased the property for $1.2 million and planned to put in about $700,000 toward renovations. Upon completion of the business plan, the property will appraise for $2.6 million on the low-end. I knew it would be a lot of work, but everything I had done to prepare was now coming into play. I was meeting people, running numbers, talking with lawyers and banks, working out schedules, and flying around the world to get it done. I was prepared and taking action and my confidence was high.

After we closed the 62-unit deal I was more excited than ever. I wanted to find my next deal as soon as possible and after meeting some more investors, I decided to get into a syndication (a process by which a person puts a property under contract and finds investors to put money into the deal to complete the purchase). I found this deal through my mentors, and they were treating it as an education platform as well. Through this syndication, I would be receiving a preferred rate of return on my investment, education on how a syndication works, more experience in apartment investing, and the ability to say I am an equity investor in another 132 units. I knew this investment was going to give me the ability to learn the process and would present more syndication opportunities soon!

The excitement of taking on a new project is exhilarating; it drives me. And the understanding of the financial freedom this will bring someday down the road is unparalleled. I now know I will have the time and ability to take my kids on vacations, take a break from work during the summers, buy the plane I've always wanted, and no longer rely on my government paycheck.

My goals are written down and I am working toward achieving them every day. Reading books like this, staying engaged in communities like ADPI, and stepping out of my comfort zone has brought me closer to my goals than I ever could have done on my own.

Mitch Durfee's Story

Every time someone mentions real estate investing, I get this rush of energy that captures me and takes me back to when I was twenty years old sitting in Al Ramadi, Iraq, dreaming of the day that I would be able to purchase real estate. That was in 2005. My interest in real estate started when my father sent me local real estate listing magazines just for light reading material. Unbeknownst to him, he was creating droplets that would become my vast ocean in the real estate industry. While other people in my unit were reading *Maxim*, I was ripping out pages of the homes I liked and made lists of renovations that would raise their values. I was creating a dream board about real estate before I knew anything about dream-boarding.

During my first deployment I saved $28,000. That was a great start, but I needed to dig deeper if I wanted to become a successful real estate investor. At the same time, knowing I had to think creatively about how to make more or save more money, I discovered the incredible opportunity that allowed me to add an additional stream of income while still in the military.

That opportunity was BAH. I now had the choice to live on post and not receive BAH or live off post and collect BAH monthly.

I also realized if I found a roommate that was also collecting BAH and we rented a place together, it would mean that we would each have extra money to spend at the bar on the weekend. Win-win! So, I started cohabitation, not even knowing I was on my way to house hacking. I just knew the numbers worked well. In fact, they worked so well that it wasn't long before we started renting the couch out just to earn a few extra bucks. Now the three of us were technically being *paid* to live off base and had more freedom than we would if we were living on post.

At the time, I was stationed at Fort Carson, Colorado, but I had no plans to stay in the service after my contract finished. If I did, I would have used my VA Loan to buy a property and rent to my roommates. I seized part of the opportunity in front of me but did not take full advantage of the strategy simply because I didn't understand all my benefits and how to use them.

Six months later, I left active duty, re-enlisted into the army reserves, and moved to Johnstown, Pennsylvania. Shortly after that, I got married and bought a house with my wife using my VA Loan. Then, my wife joined the air force and we had to relocate to Sumter, South Carolina. We were just seven months into our new mortgage, so our only option was to rent the property while we were away.

In South Carolina, I immediately started to network and ended up making friends with some like-minded folks in the air force. These guys were also using the strategy I used at Fort Carson. They were collecting BAH and renting out rooms in the same house. After a while, we realized it wasn't us who were the smart ones: the landlord was the real genius! It turns out, he was also in the military. We were paying down the mortgage principal every month and cash flowing the property for him, so he could hack *his* BAH. I remember the feeling in my stomach when it all clicked. I had a similar feeling to drinking a big milkshake and then going on a roller coaster. It was a good feeling but nauseating at the same time because I realized that he was benefiting the most.

What if I bought a house with a VA Loan, 100 percent financing, use my BAH to cover my housing payment, *and* rent out a room? Eventually, I did move back into my old house in Johnstown where I was able to rent out a room until I got deployed to Afghanistan. I was paying most of my mortgage payment by renting out a single room but was not receiving housing allowance (BAH) at the time. Imagine the extra income I would have made if I were still collecting BAH!

In 2012, I sat with my friend after a shift in Afghanistan, and my friend suggested that I do some reading. He handed me a book titled *Think and Grow Rich* by Napoleon Hill. This book had a huge impact on my life. What struck a chord in me was the supposition that I needed a means to generate passive income, or I would be working forever. Given my experience with rental house hacking and the increasing cash flow real estate provided me, I began my search for a second property. I knew people were renting properties in Colorado Springs because of the military base there, so I began searching for a cash-flowing property. As explained earlier in this book, in simple terms, the rental income generated would cover my expenses and give me a little extra cash each month.

If I found one to buy, I planned to live in the house and have my tenants pay the bills for me. So, a couple weeks later, in the back of an MRAP in Afghanistan, I put a Purchase and Sales Agreement together on a fourplex. This was the 0 percent down opportunity that I had been waiting for. I timed my leave to go home and do a final walkthrough of the property just before closing.

The fourplex started off generating $1,000 per month cash flow. I was in business. Recently, I raised the rents again and the property now produces $1,600 per month. Depending on where you are on your real estate journey, this may seem like a lot or a little. For me, an extra $1,000 dollars per month gave me some breathing room and meant that I did not have to be overseas anymore if I did not want to. To this day, I have no idea why I waited so long to get my second property. It took me four years to go from one property to five units.

After I acquired my second property, things got interesting. My eyes were focused on real estate and the potential it had to create income every single month. I left Afghanistan and decided I would buy a third property. However, when I applied for a loan, the banks told me that because I changed careers, I would not qualify to buy a property for two years, stating that they needed two years of paystubs. I refused to be disheartened and decided that if I had to wait to buy properties, I better get prepared for when they finally allow me to buy properties again.

So, in that two-year period, I started four companies, became a licensed real estate agent, and started an S-Corp for my investment properties. It was then that I also set a goal of purchasing a million dollars' worth of real estate in the next twelve months. I knew that if I owned a million dollars' worth of real estate, it would generate around $100,000 dollars a year. I had no idea how I was going to do it, but I put the goal on my phone, wrote it on my mirror, and went on Facebook Live and told my friends and family what I was going to accomplish. From there I bought, renovated, flipped, and refinanced my way toward achieving my goal. I ended up buying $1.2 million worth of property in twelve months and that momentum put me on track to owning $2.3 million worth of property just four months later.

I would like to give you a million-dollar secret here. The way I was able to double my real estate holdings in four months was through teamwork. Remember earlier in this book we talked about the power and importance of networking? To generate massive amounts of wealth in real estate, or to speed up the process, you must build what I call The Million-Dollar Team. I started off buying the properties on my own, which is why it took me so long to get my second property. Now, I have investment partners and formed a team of contractors, lenders, attorneys, property managers, and other key players. With this team, I was able to streamline the investment process. Real estate investing is a team sport. You can only go so far alone, but you can go much farther and faster with a team.

As of 2018, I purchase a new property every three to six months and own over four hundred rental units. The rental properties I own allow me to travel up to six months of the year, and I take month-long vacations to the Caribbean (which was always a dream of mine). The beautiful thing about real estate investing is you can do it from practically anywhere you have an internet connection. Because I have teams that can handle the workload while I am away, I can travel, work remotely, and I can generate income when I sleep.

I still focus on growing my companies and the real estate portfolio through partnerships. When I look back to those magazines that my dad used to send me, I never thought they would push me to where I am today. Even though my first home purchase in Johnstown, Pennsylvania, with my VA Loan was overpriced and not a great deal as an investment, I am thankful I made the purchase. It taught me valuable lessons on how to rent out a home and gave me the experience I needed to purchase more units.

After reading this far into the book you may be sitting on the edge of your chair wondering how to get started investing in real estate, but you still fear the possibility of losing money. Let me just say that, from time to time, you will purchase a property that may not be the most amazing deal. I personally write off bad deals as "tuition" but always keep my eyes strictly focused on my end goals.

You might be thinking you would get started but don't have the money. If you are just starting out, and you have a housing allowance and/or VA Loan eligibility, I would recommend contacting a real estate agent and start house hacking as soon as possible.

You might be concerned that the market is not prime and the right time to buy was after the 2008 crash. There is an old saying in real estate: The best time to buy was ten years ago, the second-best time is right now. Or my other favorite: Don't wait to buy real estate; buy real estate and wait.

If you are still hesitant but have questions or concerns that you want to be answered, find a community of like-minded investors, or reach out to my team or me. Real estate is one of those amazing things that can create a wealth stream, but you must get started. Take action now!

Nico Gibbs: Interview by Markian Sich

When did you purchase your first home and how did you find it?

Response: I closed on my first house December 17, 2013, less than six months after I graduated from the United States Merchant Marine Academy. I found the house through the MLS. I was dating a girl whose mother was a realtor in the small surf town I grew up in and she would let me look through her account. At the time, I was living with my parents. Investing has been a part of me since I was twelve years old, which is when I began investing in the stock market. I think this geared my mind a certain way that would not allow me to rent for shelter. To me, that's just throwing money away. I lived at my parents' house as a grown man at twenty-two years old for five months until I finally found the right house.

What was your experience with house hacking like?

Response: I rented out a room to a classmate of mine from the academy. It went well for the most part. For me, simple and seamless is always what works best. I offered him a flat rate for rent that included all utilities. I sold the idea to him by pointing out that he would never have to worry about a bill or his rent fluctuating. All he had to do was set up a direct deposit into my account once a month. Honestly, this benefited me because I didn't want to split bills every month. That's a headache after a while. Also, because I was bundling everything for him, I set the price of what electricity would be every month along with other bills. The only downside is that eventually he would move out into his own house and rent a room out himself. I suppose I taught him too well! The bright side was that by the time he moved out I already had another academy classmate moving into his room. It was seamless. I will say there are potential issues with renting a room out while you live in the house. "Tragedy of the commons" applies here. When you buy a house, it's your baby. You take care of every square inch the best you can. Your renters will not be as passionate about your house. You must learn how to balance this by only renting to people who will respect your property. Therefore, I always rent to people I already know. My friends went to the academy with me and have a natural tendency to be clean and orderly.

Just to bring things full circle, it's important to note my philosophy that a house is not an investment at all. An investment brings money into your life. Your house will never do that unless you rent out a room. Remember you have a liability when you buy a house until you rent out a room. We can talk about appreciation and tax credits all day but none of those bring cash into your life on a regular basis.

What is/was the best part of house hacking?

Response: Just proving your idea right. I come at this from an investor's mindset. Most people buy a house when they have enough cash to put 20 percent down and cover escrow fees. I have never paid more than 5 percent down on a house and at twenty-six I have owned two and looking to buy my third soon. There are two reasons why I don't believe in the 20 percent rule:

1. I would rather pay PMI than lock up 20 percent of my cash. I can make more with the other 15 percent by buying shares of AT&T on dividend alone then what Private Mortgage Insurance (PMI) will cost me. It makes absolutely no sense from an investor's standpoint to put down 20 percent. Also, PMI is tax deductible.

2. If you buy in the right place and at the right time you can have your house appreciate enough where that PMI will be taken off. I just did this a month ago with my second house. I bought into a townhouse community that wasn't built yet. I paid $347K for the house. By the time the last one sold at $589K, I called Wells Fargo, who owns my loan. I asked to get rid of PMI, and an appraiser found the value of my equity in my home was greater than 20 percent. So, I was able to get a new house for 5 percent down. I only paid PMI for a year and a half and still have my 15 percent working for me in the stock market.

Every time I have purchased a house, I have had people tell me: "It's not possible. You're going to become spread too thin. It's not sensible. You should put 20 percent down." I enjoy proving everyone wrong because I am doing what they are too afraid to do.

Have you ever sold or refinanced? How did that work out?

Response: I have never refinanced, and unless you bought a house prior to 2010, I wouldn't recommend it.

I sold my first house almost a year ago. It went well. Sold in forty days, didn't pay capital gains because I lived in it for two years, and I was able to write off the realtor expenses. I made $90k on the house and put it straight into the stock market.

Do you plan on buying more properties in the future?

Response: I do. I'm currently looking at a new development going up one block from my current house. It's a little bigger than my house is now at 2300 sq. ft., but it also has a workspace for commercial leasing. I want to phase into commercial real estate as I get older, and this development is offering me that smooth transition. Ideally, I live on the top two floors and the first floor will be leased out to someone. I am very excited about this one. Still not sure what my plan is for purchasing the unit, but I'll keep you updated when I decide on my plan of attack.

Do you own a property within an LLC or just in your personal name?

Response: For now, I own just in my name. Mainly because I have never had more than two properties at once. There are many benefits to an S-Corp if you buy multiple properties, but for me, there are more benefits using them as a primary and secondary home.

I come at all of this from an investor's point of view. It's important to me that I make it clear: I have only bought in cities that I truly am passionate about and believe are going to grow or hold their value. I also would never buy anything I wouldn't live in. If your aim is to buy a house with the hopes to pay it off one day, negate my advice. It's not for you. On that same note . . . you will move before you pay off your first house, I promise.

Never Sell

The idea of never selling your properties is part of a series of mindset lessons that we discuss in our Military Real Estate Investing Academy.

Ask yourself: Would you rather passively earn $10,000 every month starting in your thirties or forties, or get a lump sum of $1-2 million when you turn fifty-nine-and-a-half years of age?

There are plenty of reasons someone should or would sell an investment property. However, if you think of investing as a long-term strategy, you can develop a more secure and passive investment portfolio.

The greatest fear that real estate investors have is a market crash and a property losing its value. STOP! Passive investors do not invest for appreciation, although that is a fantastic bonus if it occurs. If you concern yourself instead with a property's *rent* potential, and you focus on the cash flow that the rent will produce, you will realize that long-term profitability stems from making a smart purchase. This makes market downturns much more manageable.

"Like the predictability of cold winter storms that show up year after year, market corrections and crashes will continue to rear their ugly heads. We've all suffered losses or know someone who has; maybe it was when the tech bubble burst in the late 1990s, when the stock market plunged in 2001, or when the housing market crashed in 2008. Those kinds of losses can shake you to your core." - Tony Robbins

One of the most important lessons Tony Robbins teaches in his fantastic book, *Unshakeable: Your Financial*

Freedom Playbook, is that after every winter, there is a spring and summer. Whenever a property loses its value due to a market crash, don't let your emotions take over. Don't be scared and sell at a loss. If you are leasing the property and your profit is more than your mortgage payment, why sell? Just wait. If the rent is higher than your mortgage plus expenses, you are *winning*. And, if the market tanks, you might even be able to refinance and get a lower interest rate, which would boost your income.

Conclusion

As billionaire industrialist Andrew Carnegie once said, "Ninety percent of all millionaires become so through owning real estate. More money has been made in real estate than in all industrial investments combined. The wise young man or wage earner of today invests his money in real estate." *Military House Hacking* aims to show you why you can't afford *not* to include real estate investing in your personal financial strategy as a service member, past or present.

The United States government has provided its military with an incredibly powerful real estate investing tool, the VA Loan. Using the earned benefit to your advantage, following VA and lender guidelines, as you PCS from duty station to duty station, can change the trajectory of your family's legacy by creating generational wealth. And it's a benefit that can be used for life, even after you separate or retire.

Whatever you do along your investing journey, stay focused on producing multiple streams of income. Real estate investing should absolutely be the base-level investment vehicle for all investors. You, the military member, veteran, spouse, or family member have a distinct advantage and we hope we can be a part of helping you reach your goals!

Action Challenge

Discover what drives you. Sit down with your spouse, friends, family, or those closest to you and discuss what gets you excited. What do you love? What would your ideal day look like if you envisioned it? That is your "why." That is what will keep you up at night and keep you moving forward.

Get educated. There are more resources today than ever before. Spend time reading, listening to podcasts and audiobooks, attend free conferences, or join our Military Real Estate Investing Academy to get started. Sometimes just base-level education can be enough to make your dreams come to life. Along the way, you'll undoubtedly network with some great people.

Join a community. Network with positive, like-minded groups and individuals who have similar ambitions, passions, and interests. Active Duty Passive Income has masterminds and meetups worldwide that can help you get started on your journey — or even take you to the next level (see our Resource page below).

Use your benefits. As stated in this book, understand how to use your hard-earned benefits as an American service member or veteran. You are among a tiny percentage of people on this earth with these distinct advantages. Why not use them?

Share and Network. Talk to your friends, family, and everyone you can about your new desire to invest in real estate. You will be surprised by how many of them might express interest in joining you or will reveal that they have already started investing in real estate as well.

If you thought the information in this book was valuable, please don't keep it a secret. Share with your fellow service members so they, too, can experience that spark!

Bonus Chapter: Step-by-Step Blueprint to Financial Success

If you want to become a financial success, first establish a solid financial foundation, one brick at a time.

As discussed already, financial literacy is a problem in the United States — and even more so in the military. There are reasons why most Americans do not have control of their finances; it's not typically taught in schools, and traditional investing and retirement principles can keep people living paycheck to paycheck.

Here are some stark statistics:

- Most Americans (77 percent) live paycheck to paycheck.
- Most Americans (57 percent) would have to go into debt to handle a $500 emergency.
- Nearly 70 percent of Americans do not even have $1,000 saved for emergencies.

This chapter will provide an actionable, step-by-step blueprint to achieve financial success by starting with the basics.

Step 1: Prepare Your Mindset

Your mindset is the most important ingredient to success! Are you stuck in the scarcity mindset? Not only are we taught to live this way, the scarcity mindset is innate; it's embedded deep in our biology as a survival tool.

Having a scarcity mindset is the concept that there are a limited number of resources that you must fight for or hoard to ensure you have what you need to survive. This type of mindset might sound like this:

- I am too overwhelmed and busy to figure out how to invest.
- Only wealthy people are able to become financially free.
- I don't know enough about the process of buying a home and it's confusing, so I shouldn't try.
- I don't have the time to learn a new skill.
- I don't know where to start, so it's not going to work for me.

Have you ever heard this inner dialogue? Or are you living with or pursuing an abundance mindset?

An abundance mindset is the concept that there is more than enough to fulfill everyone's needs and you can always create more income.

An abundance mindset might sound like this:

- I can educate myself through books, courses, and networking.
- I can find small ways to learn and connect every day.

- I have plenty of opportunities.
- I can figure out home buying, investing, and my financial future.
- There are enough resources and plenty of money available and I will figure out how to live financially free.
- I can find the time to learn a new skill.

Here are some common actions that can impact your mindset:

- Change your self-talk. Definitive words like "always" and "never" need to leave your vocabulary.
- Surround yourself with others who have an abundance mindset. Join a group that is constantly encouraging you through your growth (the ADPI community has tens of thousands of members).
- Set aside some time to learn daily. Listen to an audiobook in the car on the way to work. Begin a gratitude, prayer, or meditation practice.

These can be life-changing habits that successful people apply!

Step 2: Finding a Deep-Rooted "Why"

Many of those who have already achieved incredible financial success have:

- committed to becoming wealthy.
- decided to increase their financial education.
- committed to an abundance mindset.
- learned the concept of adding value.

Your "why" is the purpose, cause, or belief that drives you. It may sound simple, but it can be complex and multifaceted.

As current and former members of the military, we are already aware of our connection to something bigger than ourselves; a commitment to a cause and a purpose on behalf of our country.

It's your turn to choose your own *personal* "why" and work toward your own financial freedom journey. Do you want to get out of the debt? Do you want to quit the job you hate?

Why?

True freedom means living your purpose. If money was no concern, what would be the purpose, the calling, or the meaningful activity that would drive you to get up every day?

Find your "Why"

Begin exploring your "why" by asking a question behind a question.

Why do you want to make passive income?
So I can quit my job.

Why do you want to quit your job?
It's not what I was put on this earth to do.

What kind of work are you seeking?
Something more adventurous that provides security and peace.

Why do you want security and peace?
I want the world to be safe. I want to protect my loved ones and serve them by being a bastion of stability and strength.

Keep asking yourself these questions until you find your deep-rooted "why."

The importance of finding your "why"

What you focus on, expands dramatically. If you focus on putting your energy into eating better and exercising more, you can lose weight, have more energy, and be healthier. If you focus on putting more time into learning a hobby or skill, you may go from novice, to amateur, then to expert.

What gets measured, gets managed, and what gets managed, improves! This applies to all areas of your life: finances, health, education, relationships and more.

Knowing your "why" can help guide you to a path of prosperity and abundance.

Step 3: Assess Your Finances

Finding your "why" can be impactful. It's an inspiring and exciting realization once you discover it, but how do you *fulfill* your "why?"

You need a holistic, 10,000-foot view of your personal finances. You need a plan.

1. Find your exact monthly income and expenses. This is a process for creating a full picture to weigh your income vs. your expenses.

    -   Login to all your accounts: Checking and savings accounts, credit cards, retirement accounts, investments, mortgages, insurances, etc. Review or print out ALL of them to be able to start compiling the bigger picture.

    -   Alternatively, you can sign up with a service such as PersonalCapital.com or Mint.com (highly recommended, FREE software), to link all your checking, savings, credit card, and investment accounts and let it do the work for you! (Note: there are many of these types of services so please do your own research to find the one that fits you best).

Knowing your monthly income and expenses will allow you to view your total financial picture, which is often overlooked or undervalued.

2. Assess your monthly expenses going back six to twelve months to see if you spend more than you make.

3. Identify unnecessary expenses where possible.

4. Calculate your average monthly income minus expenses (net income). Write that calculation here: $_____

5. Then, write your Military Financial Freedom Number that you calculated in an earlier chapter, here: $_____

The difference between your Military Financial Freedom Number (Step 5) and your average net income (Step 4) will give you an indication of how much additional income you will need to reach financial independence.

Step 4: Creating a Path to Financial Freedom

Until you have a fully-developed passive income stream that allows you to make money while you sleep, you may need to restructure your finances and financial habits so they are working *for* you, not against you.

So where is your money really going? To get strategic about your spending, start by looking at your three highest monthly expenses:

1. Living expenses: How can you decrease your rent or mortgage?

   - Move to a less expensive location?
   - Share a room with a roommate?
   - Rent out a bedroom or storage space?
   - Military house hack with strategies learned from this book?

2. Transportation: How can you decrease your transportation costs?

   - Sell your luxury car and downgrade?
   - Decrease fuel costs?

- Decrease insurance costs?
- Rent out your car and bike, carpool, or take the bus to work.

3. Food: How can you decrease total food costs?

- Start preparing more meals at home?
- Stop buying unnecessary food items, like expensive coffee or snacks?

Evaluate what you can and are willing to do for the long-term benefits.

There may have been times when you have tried to reduce expenses but still did not find the desired result in terms of financial balance. But we urge you to dig deep. Consider the following:

- Do you have any recurring payments you didn't realize you were making?
- How much are you spending going out social events?
- Are you always the one who hosts gatherings and supplies dinner?
- Are you excessive with gifting?
- Do you spend more than you should on gadgets or online gaming?
- Do you buy designer clothing?
- Do you have idealist hobby items that rarely get used (think fancy home gym items, camping gear you only use once a year)?

There are always ways to be more frugal, but remember, there are two sides to this equation.

Instead, let's shift our focus to explore making more money!

Creating passive income is the goal and managing expenses is important, but to reach your goal you also may need to increase your *active* income.

What can you or your spouse do to increase your income?

- Side gigs/labor jobs?
- Small businesses?
- Talents you can exploit?
- Online side hustle?
- Military Real Estate Investing?

Dig deep into your finances, and you may find creative solutions to accelerate the journey.

Step 5: Analyze Your Net Worth

Once you have an overhead snapshot of your monthly financial flow, you can really get the bird's eye view of your total financial situation by evaluating your net worth.

Your net worth is an especially important metric when evaluating and growing your wealth.

As you become a more successful investor many banks will want to look at your Personal Financial Statement (PFS). A PFS is an accounting of your net worth, so it's important that you track it regularly.

Assets – Liabilities = Net Worth

Assets:

- Cash on hand
- Money in your checking or savings accounts
- Money in your investment and retirement accounts
- Equity in your primary residence or investment properties
- Equity in your vehicle (which depreciates monthly). We do not like to count this, but banks do.
- Any additional assets that hold value

Liabilities:

- Mortgage debt (on all properties)
- Credit card debt (consumer debt)
- Personal loans (car, college, etc.)
- Money borrowed from friends or family
- Any other type of debt or loans

You can calculate this number on your own, or you can use a website or platform of your choice.

What is your net worth? Is it going up or down every month?

Step 6: Make a Plan

Now that you see where your money is going every month and how it affects your net worth, you need to create a plan to:

- Pay off bad debts (liabilities)

- Create positive cash flow (assets)

Good debt, as described in detail in an earlier chapter, is anything that puts money in your pocket (like an investment property). It's an asset.

Bad debt is liability. It takes money out of your pocket each month.

List your bad debts, in order from smallest to largest balance.

For example:

- Credit card 1 = $2,588
- Credit card 2 = $7,809
- Personal loan = $8,250
- Credit card 3 = $11,752
- Auto Loan @ 6.7 percent interest = $16,654
- Student loans @ 9 percent interest = $17,770

Record your monthly payments for each debt in the space below.

Based on the difference between your income and expenses (net income), how much extra can you pay on bad debt each month? $50? $100? Or perhaps $1,000? Anything will help at the beginning. You will be adding this payment to the debt with the lowest balance. Paying off the lowest balance first will give you a sense of accomplishment and put you on a path to success.

Once that lowest debt balance is paid off, you'll add the full payment you were paying on that debt, plus the extra amount, to the next biggest debt. During this time, make minimum payments on all other debts.

You can follow this logic all the way down until you pay off the remaining bad debt.

Note: You do not need to include student debt or a mortgage in this debt-reduction strategy.

Now that you understand the bad debt reduction process, you can calculate to the month when your bad debt will be paid off.

Once complete, print this strategy out, and hang it up somewhere you will see it every day to remind you what one of your daily focus points will be.

It's also great to put a reminder of your "why" nearby so you stay motivated.

Step 7: Accelerate the Process

As you pay off bad debt, you should consider slowly building up an emergency fund. A solid goal would be to save $1,000 per person, with an end goal of 3-6 months expenses saved.

At this point, you should not invest in retirement or investment accounts. Most likely, the interest on your investments is not returning more than you are paying in interest on your debts. If so, we can reconsider this step.

Additional suggestions:

- You can find items in your home you are willing to sell, list them on Facebook Marketplace, OfferUp, LetGo, Craigslist, etc. and you will not only declutter your personal space, but you will also have more cash to pay down your debt!
- Can you pick up more shifts at work?
- Can you maximize the pay at your current job? If it's a fixed salary, how can you add more value at work to earn a promotion or raise?
- What kind of additional work can you do to earn more cash?

Step 8: Emergency Fund

Once you are out of bad debt, you should be able to finish building your emergency fund of 3-6 months' expenses in no time.

You can save in a traditional savings account or a money market account. Ask your local bank for more information. One may be more accessible (liquid) than the other, or one may have a slightly higher interest rate.

Remember, your emergency fund is not an investment account, so the interest rate isn't as crucial. This savings is a safety net, a store of reserves for a true emergency only.

Step 9: Build Your Investments

At this point, you have:

- been tracking your income and expenses.
- been tracking your net worth.
- paid off bad debt.
- built an adequate emergency fund.

How does it feel? Do you have greater peace of mind? Do you feel closer to financial freedom?

This is where the fun begins and your wealth will accumulate rapidly, because you took the time to establish a solid financial foundation.

Next, it's time to focus on investing. Depending on your goals, and which investing strategy from this book you plan to apply, you could start by saving for your first investment property.

Many people will want to invest their money as soon as possible. Maybe once they have $1,000 saved, $5,000 saved, or maybe even $25,000.

Let's compare:

If you saved $1,000 and invested in the stock market, and if it generated 8 percent interest annually, and you held it in that account for a period of five years, your return on investment would be almost $500.

If you did the same with $5,000, your return on investment would be close to $2,500. It's the same return on investment, but it feels a little better, right?

Now, if you invested $100,000 at that same 8 percent annual interest rate, your return over five years would be almost $50,000!

There is extreme power in compound interest, so while investing in the stock market may not be your ultimate goal, it's one strategy of many on the road to financial freedom.

You may choose to invest in stocks, bonds, commodities, cryptocurrency, real estate, or other investment vehicles.

If you learn to invest in income-producing assets, you, like thousands before you, can achieve financial freedom.

For those of you ready to move to the next level, visit our platform for the free Blueprint to Financial Success worksheet.

www.activedutypassiveincome.com/resources

Bonus Chapter: The Credit Guide

Simple, Actionable Steps to Repair, Improve, and Maintain your Credit Score

The purpose of this chapter is to share easy and effective methods to repair, improve, and maintain your credit score. If these principles are properly applied, the result could put you in a better position to accomplish your financial goals.

The information in this book is always relevant, but can be most useful when:

- preparing to purchase or refinance a home.
- applying for a job.
- applying to rent or buy a home.
- applying for a car loan.

What is a Credit Score?

A credit score is a number ranging from 300 to 850. The score indicates a person's credit worthiness and can be used by debtors to define how likely someone is to repay debt. It is also referred to as a FICO Score, which stands for Fair Isaac Corporation. FICO was the original company to offer a credit-risk model that resulted in a numerical score, but there are three main credit reporting agencies (CRAs, also known as credit bureaus), that gather, store, and report your credit information.

Lenders and other financial institutions rely on these three main credit bureaus when looking to pull and review your credit reports:

- Experian (https://www.experian.com/)
- TransUnion (https://www.transunion.com)
- Equifax (https://www.equifax.com/)

Although these are the three most used credit reporting agencies (CRAs), there are numerous CRAs in the business. Consumer credit history, numerical scores, and detailed credit reports are important to understand, so we want to ensure you have some basic knowledge before we dive in to strategies.

The table below shows a general breakdown of how the agencies and debtors may view your credit score:

580-669	Fair	17 percent of the population
670-739	Good	21 percent of the population
740-799	Very Good	25 percent of the population
800-850	Exceptional	21 percent of the population

As you can see from the table above, your number correlates to how your credit worthiness is viewed. Typically, if your score is above 720, you will get great rates on most loans and credit cards. If it falls into the category above 760 (this is your target!), you will get the best rates on all loans and credit cards. This is because lenders will see you as a low-risk borrower.

The scoring system considers the previous two years of credit activity but can include important information from within the last ten years.

What impacts your credit score?

Although there are dozens of ways to lower your credit score, there are only five major categories that directly impact your score:

1.   On-time payments (35 percent of your score)

It has never been easier to ensure all your credit accounts and installment loans are paid on time, every time, with the use of technology and automated payment plans.

Do not miss a payment! You should always make your minimum monthly payment or more.

To maximize the benefit to your credit, make your automatic payment at least three days prior to the statement due date. This way, if the credit bureau checks your account the day the payment is due, the payment has already processed, and the account will show a zero balance.

One late payment on an account can default to an extremely high interest rate on a card (25-30 percent interest).

Alternatively, monthly payments made to your accounts on time, can increase your score as much as four to five points per account.

2. Credit Utilization/Credit-to-Debt Ratio (10-30 percent of your score)

The key here is to have as high a credit limit as possible on three or four different types of cards (Visa, American Express, MasterCard, Discover, etc.).

The higher the limit, the lower your overall percentage of usage will be as you use it. Imagine using $800 of revolving credit on a card that only has a $1,000 total limit. Here, you are using 80 percent of the total limit, which will negatively affect your credit score.

Conversely, imagine using $800 of revolving credit on a card that has a $10,000 total limit. Here, you are only using only 8 percent of the total limit.

This can make a substantial difference in the eyes of the three major credit bureaus.

Action Item:

Call your credit card company to request a limit increase if needed (you can do this every 90 days).

Sample call:

Financial Institution	You
Why are you calling for the increase?	I would like to improve my credit score.
How much would you like to increase it?	As high as possible. (If they ask for a number, say, $50,000.)
Why should we approve you? (It is unlikely they will ask this.)	I am very responsible with my credit and would like to get my score above 760 as soon as possible.
Is there anything else we can do for you today?	Yes, can you please **lower my interest rate** as low as possible?

Tips:

- Keep amounts owed less than 30 percent of the total credit limit per card.
- Never pay interest. The secret is to pay the statement balance in full, every month, if possible. Do not pay the total balance, just the *statement* balance.
- Try to pay more than the minimum monthly payment, otherwise you will accumulate additional interest.
- A HELOC (Home Equity Line of Credit) is a line of credit that is viewed similarly to a credit

144

card (revolving account) on your report. Ask your lender to report it as a mortgage (installment account).

- Avoid consumer credit cards (such as Macy's, Target, Shell, or any department store). They are tempting because of the "save 10-20 percent now" lure, but they do not positively impact your credit score like major credit card accounts.

  If you have opened one or more of these, do not cancel your account — simply pay off your balance, use it once a year, and pay off the statement balance in full immediately. In the future, avoid applying for consumer credit cards.

3. Length of Credit History (15 percent of your score)

Do not close any accounts.

Keep all your old accounts open and in good standing. At this point, it is best to use them occasionally and pay off the statement balance in full. Or, set up one of your older accounts to pay a utility bill or other small payment.

Accounts five or more years old with a $5,000 limit are the most secure accounts and will have the highest positive impact on your credit score.

Bonus tip: Become an authorized user on a trusted family or close friend's most secure, oldest account.

This can potentially increase your credit score by 45-50 points in as few as forty-five days.

You will not need to use their account; they just need to maintain their positive usage and payment history and you will gain from that.

Ensure the person you are asking is financially responsible, prior to asking them for this favor.

4. Types of Credit Used (10 percent of your score)

Installment loans: Auto loans can show very little to no score increase even with on-time payment history and/or paying off the debt. Mortgage loans, however, can have a significant impact after every six months of on-time payments. Both, however, will destroy credit fast if not paid on time.

We are not suggesting getting as many installment loans as possible, but these accounts are a bit more important to ensure payments are made on time and in full every month.

5. Credit Bureau Inquiries (10 percent of your score)

Inquiries to your credit bureaus to check your FICO score, can be soft inquiries or hard inquiries.

Soft Inquiry: An inquiry that occurs when a person or company checks your credit report (background check, advertising, jobs, etc.)

When you check your credit score soft inquiries can occur without your permission, but do not worry, they should not negatively affect your credit.

Hard Inquiry: An inquiry that occurs when a prospective lender checks your credit report to make a lending decision.

Hard inquiries can slightly lower your credit score and will typically stay on your report for two years.

An example of a hard inquiry is a pre-approval for a mortgage loan application. When a mortgage lender pre-approves you for a loan, it typically results in a drop on your credit score. The loan officer will request your Social Security Number and are required to tell you when they are running your credit to process and finalize the loan application.

Action Items:

Go to https://www.optoutprescreen.com. Opt out of "0 percent financing for a limited time" offers that come through the mail. Opt out permanently, print out, sign, and mail in the authorization page to all three bureaus. Within approximately forty-five days, your credit score should increase by 10 points, because the credit bureaus recognize you are opting out of potentially hazardous offers.

Once you have reached your credit score goals, search for the best rewards credit cards to take advantage of your good credit. American Express waives their annual fee ($450) for military service members. If this applies to you, call them, and consider applying for the Platinum Card to receive tremendous benefits.

Lastly, if your credit reports contain findings that are accurate but negative, write to your creditors and ask them to remove the bad information right away. Be polite, as they are not required to comply with your request. We have provided four sample letters below and instructions on which ones to use and when to use them.

A Step-by-Step Guide on How to Identify and Dispute Errors on Your Credit Report (even if it is your fault)

As explained previously, you should download and use a free monitoring service, or see if your bank or credit card company may have one available.

Request your free credit reports from all three credit bureaus at annualcreditreport.com. You can do this every year.

Review your credit report line by line. Look for anything unusual.

Highlight any errors or unusual items you may want to dispute. This includes anything you do not want on your credit report, even if it is your fault. For example:

- Foreclosures
- Thirty-, sixty-, ninety-day late notices
- Collections
- Bankruptcies

Then follow the steps below to send the dispute letters to the respective credit bureau that reported the error, along with the following attachments:

- Copy of driver's license
- Copy of utility bill
- Copy of social security card

Overview of the Dispute Letters

Letter 1: Send to Credit Bureaus (TransUnion, Equifax, and Experian)

This letter will initiate a dispute investigation.

- Fill out the form and mail it in.
- Due to the Fair Credit Reporting Act, you can request proof from the bureaus that you were late on a payment (even if you know you were). If they return proof that you were late/unpaid, there are no legal ramifications. If it was your fault, the goal here is to send the letter. If they do not respond with proof from the creditor within thirty days, it can be removed from your credit report.

Letter 2: Send to Creditors (i.e., Best Buy, a collection agency, Chase Bank, Target, etc.)

- Send this letter at the same time as Letter 1.
- Ask for documentation from the creditors proving you were late, foreclosed on, or took bankruptcy, etc. They cannot send a computer printout; it must be the actual proof, i.e., copy of bill or contract to pay.
- Once completed, after approximately thirty days, you should automatically receive a copy of your credit report with the results of the investigation. The report will say either DELETED or VERIFIED. If it says DELETED, the process is complete. If it says VERIFIED, you must send Letter 3.

Letter 3: Second Letter to the Credit Bureaus (only send if Letter 2 results are VERIFIED, with or without proof)

This letter will be sent back to the three credit bureaus and the legal department of the creditor. More than likely, no proof will be provided.

If proof is provided, send Letter 4.

Letter 4: Credit Bureau (last resort)

If a creditor sends a letter back to the bureau verifying the debt is yours, send Letter 4.

It would be shocking to get to this point. If it was a true error, this letter should correct it. If it was your fault, this letter may remove it anyway.

Letter Templates

Letter 1
Download Letter 1: https://bit.ly/CreditLetter1
MM/DD/YYYY

NAME
Your Home Address
Your Email Address
Your Phone Number

Choose one of the following as it corresponds with the discrepancy:

Customer Service
Equifax Information Services
P.O. Box 740241
Atlanta, GA 30374)

Customer Service
Experian Information Services
P.O. Box 2002
Allen, Texas 75013

Customer Service
Transunion
1561 E. Orangethorpe Avenue
Ste 100
Fullerton, CA 92831

I, (Insert Name), am personally forwarding you the attached request for a corrected credit report.

I request the following items be immediately investigated, because they are inaccurate:

1. Company Name:
   - My Account Number:
   - Discrepancy:

2. Company Name:

   - My Account Number:
   - Discrepancy:

3. Company Name:
   - My Account Number:
   - Discrepancy:

Please notify me when the items have been deleted.

You may send an updated copy of my credit report to my home address listed above.

Also, please send me the names and addresses of individuals you contacted so I may follow up.

Thank you so much.
Best regards,

(Insert Name)

Letter 2

Download Credit Letter #2:
https://bit.ly/CreditLetter2

MM/DD/YYYY

NAME
Your Home Address
Your Email Address
Your Phone Number

Account #:

Creditor Name

Creditor Address

Your company has sent a letter to the Credit Bureaus alleging verification that I was delinquent with a collection debt that I owed to you.

I believe this allegation to be an error.

I would like you to send me the proof of delinquency, assuming it exists, in accordance with the FDCPA sections 809a & b.

Please send me:
1. Copies of all original documents and/or contracts that prove this debt.

2. All records that prove the late payment history.

3. Proof that the interest charge is legal and a part of the original contract.

4. Proof that you did not violate the FDCPA section, 807 #8 through your previous letter to the credit agencies.

5. Proof that the date of occurrence (last payment) is correct as reported to the credit agencies.

Pending the outcome of my investigation of any evidence that you submit, you are instructed to take no action that could be detrimental to any of my credit reports.

Thank you for your cooperation.

Best regards,

(Insert Name)

Letter 3

Download Credit Letter #3:
https://bit.ly/CreditLetter3

MM/DD/YYYY

NAME
Your Home Address
Your Email Address
Your Phone Number

Choose one of the following as it corresponds with
the discrepancy:

Customer Service
Equifax Information Services
P.O. Box 740241
Atlanta, GA 30374)

Customer Service
Experian Information Services
P.O. Box 2002
Allen, Texas 75013

Customer Service
Transunion
1561 E. Orangethorpe Avenue
Ste 100
Fullerton, CA 92831

RE: Demand for Corrected Credit Report

To whom it may concern:

On (Insert Date), I wrote to tell you to verify the items I had identified as inaccurate or incomplete in my credit report.

Copies of my correspondence are attached for your review.

Since you have not given me names of persons you contacted for verification of the information, nor have you complied within the statutory time period (thirty days) to my request for verification, I assume that you have not been able to verify the information I have disputed.

Therefore, you must comply with the provisions of the Fair Credit Reporting Act, and drop the disputed items from my credit report.

I request you send me a copy of my updated credit report showing the elimination of the items that I disputed on the attached letters.

This copy must be provided free, according to 15 USC section 1681j. I request that it be postmarked within five days after signing the certified mail receipt for the letter you are holding.

If I do not receive an updated copy of my credit report with the disputed items dropped, my attorney will pursue my legal rights under 15 USC section 1681 of the Fair Credit Reporting Act, "Civil liability for willful noncompliance."

Your credit bureau may be liable for:

1) Any actual damages I sustain by your failure to delete the items,

2) Punitive damages as the court may allow, and

3) Costs of the court action, plus attorney's fees.

Thank you for your cooperation.

Sincerely,

(Insert Name)

Letter 4

Download Credit Letter #4:
https://bit.ly/CreditLetter4

MMM DD YYYY

NAME
Your Home Address
Your Email Address
Your Phone Number

Choose one of the following as it corresponds with the discrepancy:

Customer Service
Equifax Information Services
P.O. Box 740241
Atlanta, GA 30374)

Customer Service
Experian Information Services
P.O. Box 2002
Allen, Texas 75013

Customer Service
Transunion
Ste 100
1561 E. Orangethorpe Avenue
Fullerton, CA 92831

Account #

To whom it may concern:

I am writing to dispute the account referenced

above. I have disputed this account information as inaccurate with you and you have returned correspondence to me and stated you were able to verify these debts.

How is this possible?

Under the laws of the FDCPA, I have contacted the ALLEGED CREDITORS myself and they have been unable to verify the information they are reporting to you; they have not even verified that these are indeed my debts.

I enclosed copies of my requests to the creditors, asking them to validate my debts.

These debts are not mine and I was given no evidence of my obligation to pay these debts to these creditors.

The FCRA requires you to verify the validity of the item within thirty days. If the validity cannot be verified, you are obligated by law to remove the item.

There is a clear case of unverified debt here, and I urge you to remove this item before I am forced to take legal action.

I request that you send me a copy of my updated credit report showing the elimination of the items mentioned above. This copy must be provided free, according to 15 USC section 1681j. I request that it be postmarked within five days after signing the certified mail receipt for the letter you are holding.

If I do not receive an updated copy of my credit report with the disputed items dropped, my attorney will pursue my legal rights under 15 USC section 1681n of the Fair Credit Reporting Act, "Civil liability for willful noncompliance."

Your credit bureau may be liable for:

1. Any actual damages I sustain by your failure to delete the items

2. Defamation

3. Violation of the Fair Credit Reporting Act

4. Punitive damages as the court may allow

5. Costs of the court action, plus attorney's fees

Thank you for your cooperation.

Best regards,

(Insert Name)

Additional Resources

Website:
www.activedutypassiveincome.com

Community:
www.militaryrealestateinvesting.com

Education/Courses (residential and commercial):
www.activedutypassiveincome.com/education

Financial Services (military real estate agents, lenders and more):
www.activedutypassiveincome.com/connect

Blog:
www.activedutypassiveincome.com/blog/

Free Resources:
www.activedutypassiveincome.com/resources

Acknowledgements

A special thank you to Pam Watts for her many hours spent on the phone helping with editing and formatting.

Spencer Thomas, Victoria Wester-Griggs, Jill Campbell, Adrianne Phillips, Aladino Perez, Allysa Wray, Allyson Kelly, Arabia Littlejon, Brandon Elder, Buddy Rushing, Catherine Livingstone, Chad Payton, Cheyenne Foster, Chris Coker, Cindy Byler, Dan Dwyer, David & Tasha Gwilt, Dustin Nguyen, Erik Clark, Jaime Soto, Jarred Martin, Juan Ramirez, Kateryna Sich, Lauryn Carr, Matthew Cole, Matthew Parker, Mike Chiesl, Mike Murray, Nataly Sich, Nico Gibbs, Raquel La Barr, Rod Khleif, Ruth Paik, Ryan Hebron, Scott Hatzung, Sean Taylor, Stephen Anderson, Talia Upchurch, Tyler Gibson, Vasyl Bilokonsky, Wayne Bemet.

Thank you. Your help spreading the word and supporting the ADPI team during and after the launch of this book was invaluable.

www.ingramcontent.com/pod-product-compliance
Lightning Source LLC
LaVergne TN
LVHW052027080426
835513LV00018B/2204